Caroline Atwater Mason

A Minister of the World

Caroline Atwater Mason

A Minister of the World

ISBN/EAN: 9783744710794

Printed in Europe, USA, Canada, Australia, Japan

Cover: Foto ©ninafisch / pixelio.de

More available books at **www.hansebooks.com**

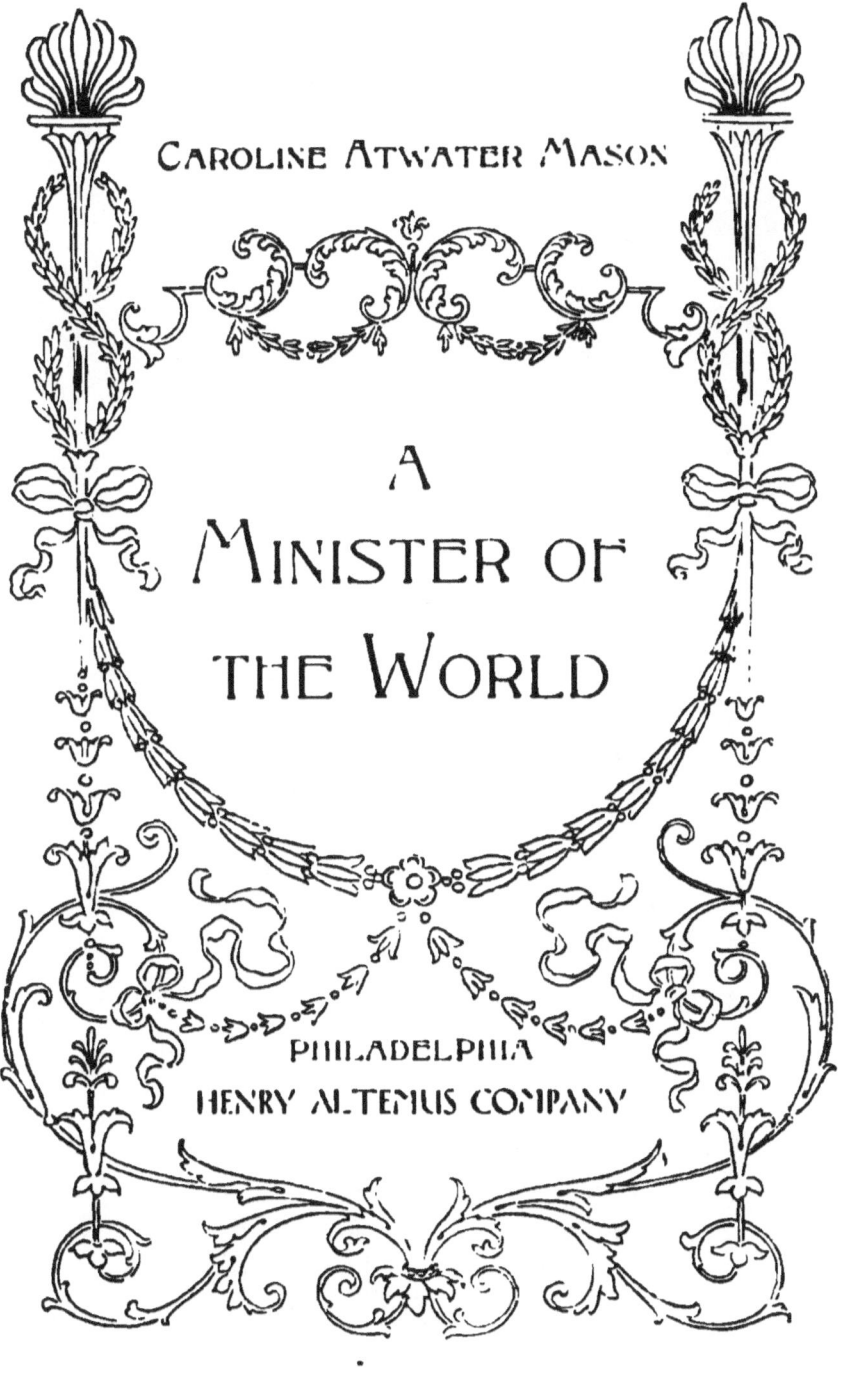

Caroline Atwater Mason

A Minister of the World

Philadelphia
Henry Altemus Company

" Take any of the sons our Age has nursed,
Fed with her food and taught her best and worst;
Suppose no great disaster; look not nigh
On hidden hours of his extremity;
But watch him like the flickering magnet stirred
By each imponderable look and word,
And think how firm a courage every day
He needs to bear him on life's common way,
Since even at the best his spirit moves
Thro' such a tourney of conflicting loves, —
Unwisely sought, untruly called untrue;
Beloved and hated and beloved anew;
Till in the changing whirl of praise and blame
He feels himself the same and not the same,
And often, overworn and overwon,
Knows all a dream and wishes all were done.

I know it, such an one these eyes have seen
About the world, with his unworldly mien,
And often idly hopeless, often bent
On some tumultuous deed and vehement,
Because his spirit he can nowise fit
To the world's ways and settled rule of it,
But thro' contented thousands travels on
Like a sad heir in disinherison,
And rarely by great thought or brave emprise
Comes out above his life's perplexities,
Looks through the rifted cloudland, and sees clear
Fate at his feet and the high God anear."

       FREDERIC W. H. MYERS.

ILLUSTRATIONS.

Wherever he turned his eyes that morning
    he saw the one face . . . . *Frontispiece*

"You will excuse me, perhaps, if I do not
    rise" . . . . *To face page* 23

She was the young lady who was most
    intently observed . . . . "   36

"There ought to be a kind of invisible
    affinity between us". . . . . "   50

Across the room, Stephanie Loring was
    the centre of a group . . . . "   84

As the light of the lamp struck upward in
    her face, he recognized Emily Merle . "   119

Emily joins them, and the women meet
    with unaffected kindness . . . . . "   150

A MINISTER OF THE WORLD

I.

> 'T was one of the charmed days
> When the genius of God doth flow,
> The wind may alter twenty ways,
> A tempest cannot blow;
> It may blow north, it still is warm;
> Or south, it still is clear;
> Or east, it smells like a clover-farm;
> Or west, no thunder fear.
>
> EMERSON.

THERE is a row of locust-trees in front of the parsonage at Thornton, on the outer edge of the sidewalk; and it seemed, on this particular June afternoon, as if all the upper spaces of the air were occupied by the fragrance of their pale, wind-blown blossoms. Below, on our own level, was the spicy breath of the garden roses and the honest, heavy sweetness of the syringa. But the fragrance of the locust-blossoms has a peculiarly aërial, elusive quality, in fact, a certain loftiness, as if it knew that its family had seen better days and was not held in the high regard of an earlier time, and hence it would not descend to delight the sense of the sordid folk with free bestowal. Still more delicate and more elusive was the scent of the grape-vine blossom; but this was shyness without the assumption of superiority. It was forever coming to you from around a corner, but if you went to the corner to catch it, it would have escaped you. All of these precious odors, and I dare not say how many more, were making the air around the parsonage intoxicating that early afternoon.

The house was a white cottage with a wide front and a small veranda on which the house door stood open directly into the sitting-room. There was a cleanly swept, home-woven carpet on the floor of this room, a table with a red cotton cover; and on a white painted shelf, between two vases filled with garden flowers, a clock ticked with sharp emphasis from its Gothic wooden case. The emptiness and orderliness of the room, the open door, the very silence itself, seemed to impart a sense of expectancy, but no one was to be seen. Outside, the bees hummed drowsily in the yellow roses which were dazzlingly bright in the broad sunshine; a light breeze passed now and then over the grass, which grew as high as the palings of the fence on either side of the walk. It was already ripe for the scythe, for there had been an early spring in Thornton. Fairly swamped in the tall timothy stood deep-red peonies, their petals dropping and drifting heedlessly around them in the sea-green depths of the grass. Standing on the walk between the clumps of peonies one could look down across the clover-fields which adjoined the parsonage acre and see the lovely Thornton valley, with its smooth green meadows, its graceful elm-trees dotted along the river's bank, and the wooded slopes of the enclosing hills. Beyond the parsonage, as one looked up the village street, stood the white church with its square, ungraceful tower, and its uncompromising austerity of outline. A row of maple-trees grew before it, concealing the village from view. But there was not much to conceal. Thornton was only a cluster of houses, each a farmhouse in its way, with a church, a post-office, a store, and a blacksmith's shop, to supply the actual needs of the surrounding neighborhood. For those who confessed to complex and ambitious demands there was Pembroke, the county-seat, only seven miles away, where were to be found all the refinements and luxuries of life. But Pembroke with its noise of locomotives and factories was well out of sight and hearing, and Thornton dozed on in its dreamy stillness, undisturbed thus far, even by the advent of the " summer boarder," an unconscious, unspoiled, country village.

Down the street a light open wagon containing two women, one of whom was driving the somewhat spiritless horse, could now be seen approaching the parsonage. The clock on the white shelf had just drawn up all its vibrations into a single distinct effort and clanged out two resonant strokes. A slender gray-haired woman in a checked cotton gown and white apron came out to the door just as the clock struck, and stood watching the horse and wagon as they drew near.

"It's Aunt Lecty and Elizy, I declare!" she exclaimed in a shrill but gentle voice. "They've got here first of all!"

There was silence in the house as before, and after a moment's pause the woman stepped back within the room, and addressing herself toward a door which stood open on the left, she cried:

"Stephen, don't you hear what I say? Lecty Wescott's bringing Aunt Elizy; they've turned in already, and you must hurry and help her to get out of the wagon."

In the room beyond, at an oblong table covered with green enamelled cloth, a young man was sitting in his shirt-sleeves with his back to the door, writing. The room was not a large one, and its walls were nearly lined with bookshelves, rising two-thirds of the distance to the low ceiling. Above the books, facing the door, hung a photograph of Holman Hunt's "Light of the World."

On being thus appealed to, the young man rose from the table, stretched one long arm up behind the door and produced a coat which he drew on as he crossed the sitting-room with a few strides and followed the woman, who was his mother, out through the clean, sunny kitchen, to the horse-block at the side of the house. He was a tall, athletic fellow, this Stephen Castle, looking less than his eight and twenty years, with light hair close cropped, a finely browned skin, and a pair of good gray eyes. There was about him in rare degree that indefinable personal attraction which gives charm to every word and motion of some men and women. His face wore the stamp of thought and study, and indeed there was upon it a suggestion of spiritual purity and earnestness, which united with the boyish freedom of his movements and his thoroughgoing manliness, to make a peculiarly winning personality, even to one who saw him only for a moment. He was the pastor of the church in Thornton, and had been for four years, coming thither direct from the Divinity School. With him came his mother, a widow, who, having no other child, followed him wherever he went, making a home for him and devoting herself to him and his interests absolutely. Mrs. Castle had been country born and bred herself, and Stephen had pursued his studies in the humbler and more rural schools of New England, so that neither of them felt anything of deprivation or sacrifice in settling in a little village like Thornton and adapting themselves to the ways of a farming parish. Indeed, Stephen Castle would not have believed then that he could have been in his element in a city church. He doubted whether he was man enough to preach to this handful of country folk; he had not learned his own powers yet; his weaknesses he thought he clearly understood.

Four years were not needed, even with the slow and unenthusiastic habit of New England country people, to win for the young pastor the almost adoring love of his parishioners. They petted and praised him; boasted of him wherever they went; treasured and repeated the things he said, as men do the sayings of a darling child; gloried in his physical and intellectual strength, and yet more in his obvious weaknesses; and, in fine, idolized him and spoiled him as far as this kind of devotion could spoil. Stephen was of too fine a nature to become vain or assuming; if he grew somewhat imperious, it was in so fine a degree that it merely served to attract men and women more irresistibly to him.

He stood now on the rough stone block before the kitchen door and lifted the little old lady whom his mother called "Aunt Elizy" from the wagon as easily as if she had been a child, then holding her withered, chilly little hands in his, which were warm and steady, he looked with a deference which sat well upon him into her face and said:

"It was very good of you to come, Aunt Eliza; you don't know how glad and proud you make us."

The old lady was dressed in a black silk gown and an old-fashioned fringed mantilla.

She wore a large black bonnet, under which appeared the snow-white crinkled frill of her cap, and some soft gray hair. Her face was fairly tiny and much wrinkled, but sensitive and refined in its expression, and the hazel eyes had almost the brightness of young eyes, as she looked up with a certain archness, which in some women lasts a lifetime, and said:

"Then why don't you kiss me, Stephen?"

At this the middle-aged woman who still sat in the wagon, threw back her head and laughed.

"If you don't beat all, Aunt Elizy," she exclaimed. "I'd never have brought you down here if I'd s'posed you were goin' to perform like this. Mis' Castle, I shouldn't think you'd stand there and allow such goin's on!"

Quite regardless of her noisy banter, Stephen bent and gravely kissed the little lady, and then drawing her hand into his arm he carefully led her up the steps and into the house. It was only the door of a very humble country parsonage, but the young man's chivalrous courtesy, and the old lady's quiet grace and fine manner would have been in place at the entrance to a royal house.

II.

>   . . . And yet I knew a maid,
> A young enthusiast, who escaped these bonds;
> Her eye was not the mistress of her heart;
> Far less did rules prescribed by passive taste,
> Or barren, intermeddling subtleties,
> Perplex her mind. . . .
> Whate'er the scene presented to her view,
> That was the best, to that she was attuned
> By her benign simplicity of life,
> And through a perfect happiness of soul.
>   WORDSWORTH.

ONE after another, at longer or shorter intervals, half-a-dozen carriages were now driven into the parsonage yard, and their owners were received by Mrs. Castle and conducted to her own bedroom. Having laid aside their bonnets and frowned for an instant at their front hair in the looking-glass, they crossed the large and rather empty sitting-room and entered the parlor, where chairs and tables had been pushed to the wall to leave all the middle space free for the quilting-frame, on which was stretched a marvellous piece of Mrs.

Castle's handiwork constructed of small cotton squares of nearly every color united by bands of white.

"Ain't it a beauty?"

"There don't anything beat Irish chain, does there, Mis' Castle?"

"What if we should spoil it in the quiltin'? I'm most afraid to touch it, it is so handsome."

These and many kindred exclamations were made as the guests entered the cool parlor and took the places assigned them by Mrs. Castle around the quilting-frame. Aunt Eliza alone did not join the party, but sat in state in a high-backed, haircloth-covered easy-chair, with a little white knitting-work in her hands. More gently born and bred than her neighbors, being a fine illustration of the "old school" type of woman, Aunt Eliza's presence was greatly desired in the Thornton gatherings as imparting something of distinction. Her advanced age and increasing feebleness, however, generally served as sufficient reason for refusing all invitations, hence Mrs. Castle's "quilting" was held to be highly favored, and many admiring remarks were made to the effect that "Aunt Elizy was just as smart as ever," and that "she would n't have come anywheres else only to the parsonage, but of course she knew it would please Mr. Castle, and wa' n't it a sight to see how attentive he was to her? And to hear her call him Stephen!" The story of the kiss at the kitchen door was speedily set in circulation and awakened a vast amount of subdued hilarity, of the form considered suitable to a party at the parsonage. As "Lecty," or Mrs. Wescott, the niece of Aunt Eliza who had accompanied her, confided to her right-hand neighbor at the quilt:

"It ain't goin' to do to train too hard when you come to the minister's house."

The disposition to "train," however, was not to be wholly suppressed, and presently Mrs. Wescott remarked, with a peculiarly mischievous glance at a fair-haired girl in a white gown who had come with her mother and was quilting demurely at her side, —

"I don't know what the rest thinks, and I don't hardly dare to say anything before Mis' Castle, but after all it does strike me that there's something awful suspicious about this quilt." Then looking over her shoulder she cried in mock consternation: "Oh, my gracious, the Elder ain't nowheres about, is he?"

A Minister of the World

"Why, Lecty, what do you mean?" asked one of the women.

"Don't ask me, I don't dare to say another word; Mis' Castle looks so sober I'm scared, and if the Elder heard me he might turn me out of meetin'. But there's one thing about it," she cried, the sense of fun flashing from her black eyes, "if he does, I'll just tell the deacons I saw him kissin' Aunt Elizy outside the kitchen door, right under them old locust-trees, with my own eyes!" And at this she burst into a hearty fit of laughter in which everybody joined, — everybody, that is, except Aunt Eliza. She was not known to have laughed aloud since her husband died twenty years ago.

"But what is it you mean, Lec, about this quilt being suspicious?" asked the hostess, when the laughter had subsided. "I am sure I don't understand."

"Oh, now, Mis' Castle, don't you be too innocent. You know I always speak right out and say what all the rest thinks. It ain't to be supposed that our minister is goin' to live single all his days, when every girl between Thornton Four Corners and Pembroke is makin' eyes at him, and I don't know's I wonder any; I'd

A Minister of the World

make eyes at him myself if 't would be any use, — that is, if Hiram had n't any objections," she added, with a quaint wit which made her the leader of conversation in all the Thornton gatherings. "When folks go to makin' quilts," she went on, soberly, "when it's very well known that they have a whole shelf full put away already, why it begins to look as if—" here she paused in pretended embarrassment.

"Looks as if what, Lec? Go on!" was the general cry.

"Well," she said, with a toss of her head, "I ain't sure myself that it's proper for Liny Barry to be workin' on this quilt. I've noticed the Elder likes her singin' pretty well lately, have n't you, Mis' Sanford?"

A shriek of laughter greeted this sally, and the young girl thus alluded to blushed rosy red and bent lower over her needle, her mother, a dignified, matronly woman, seeming not at all displeased at this form of attack, which she judged it best, however, not to prolong too far. Turning to Mrs. Castle, she said:

"I put a basket of doughnuts under the seat of our buggy when we came away. I don't know whether Mr. Castle took them out, but I meant him to."

A Minister of the World

While Mrs. Castle was expressing her gratitude, the company at the quilt were joining in a chorus of praise of Mrs. Barry's doughnuts, which it appeared were famous throughout Thornton, and the despair of all the other housewives, who lamented that they "could n't give them just the twist, and turn them out just so light and soft and yellow as Drusilly could."

Meanwhile, Stephen Castle, whose doings and sayings and preferences were directly or indirectly the subject of most of the conversation in the parlor, had again laid aside his coat, borrowed a scythe of his nearest neighbor, and was now hard at work mowing the tall timothy in the front yard. Of the women gathered around the quilt, Lina Barry alone had discovered this fact, and through the half-closed shutters of one parlor window she was enjoying all to herself the sight of the athletic grace of motion with which the young minister performed this labor, which to her seemed so far beneath him.

Down on his knees, Stephen was pulling out the grass close to the crimson peonies which he could not cut with the scythe without beheading the flowers, when a clear voice behind him said:

"I should think you would get a lawn-mower, and try to make it look nice here, Mr. Castle. It has been dreadful, the way you have let that grass grow."

Turning his head slightly, the young man greeted the speaker by waving a handful of grass toward her.

"You will excuse me, perhaps, if I do not rise," he said, briefly. "I am crushed by your severity, Emily."

"Oh, no, you are not!" the girl retorted gayly. "You are only trying to gain time to defend yourself."

Upon this, Stephen sprang to his feet and turned full upon her.

"What an absurd idea," he exclaimed, "that I should try to make a fashionable, sheared lawn of my old dooryard! I should hate it if it tried to look like something it could never be. I love this tall, waving timothy, and besides, I am too good a farmer to waste so much good hay with Doll there in the barn to eat it."

The girl before him laughed merrily at the energy of his defence.

"You got out of it better than I expected," she returned; then holding out her hands which were full of books, "See," she said, "I have brought your books back. Where shall I leave them?"

"Oh, yes; why, in the study, if you will, for my mother has cleared out the sitting-room for the company tea, you know."

"I will find their places on the book-shelves, if you like. I think I know where they belong."

"Thanks. Do so."

And Stephen again lifted his scythe, while Emily Merle passed, light of foot and heart, into the parsonage. She was a slender girl, with dark hair and eyes, not strikingly pretty, but noticeable for her bright and joyous look, and the frank, spirited self-reliance which was conveyed in her voice and expression. There was no meek adoring in her eyes as they met Stephen Castle's, but rather a challenge which, although playful, was sufficient to put him on his mettle. Plainly it did not suit him to have this clear-eyed young woman suspect him of laziness.

Entering the study alone, Emily hesitated a moment, yielding to an unconquerable shyness. In spite of herself this room seemed a kind of shrine into which she scarcely dared to enter without its master. On the writing-table lay several broad sheets of manuscript written in a bold handwriting which she recognized. She was afraid she might read the very words of the next Sabbath's sermon, and that would have seemed to her like an almost profane intrusion upon holy things.

She crossed quickly to the book-shelves, and stood before them trying to see the spaces where the books belonged which she had brought. The room was almost dusky, the grape-vines grew so closely about the open windows, with their thick, green shade, and the air was strangely sweet. As she stood, intently looking, she was aware of the vine being pushed aside, and Stephen Castle's face appeared outside the window.

Emily could not control the quick color which rose in her cheeks, but without turning her head she said, quietly:

"I see where the Saint Augustine belongs, — on the upper shelf, and the Martineau, here, of course," and then she hesitated.

"Put the 'Natural Law' down on my desk, if you will, I shall want it to refer to. Did you like it?" Stephen asked.

"Yes, although I am afraid it is not all true. But, do you know, I think you have marked it so oddly? Some of the parts which I call weak you have marked for especial power."

"Show me one, please."

"I can't now. I am going in the other room to quilt. That is what I came for, you know."

"Never mind the quilting. I want you to bring the book over here and let me see what you mean."

Stephen Castle said these words in a tone which Emily found it hard to resist, although she had an instinctive feeling that she ought not to be lingering in the study, but in a moment their heads were bending together over the book which lay on the window-sill between them, and the sunlight sifted down through the leaves upon its pages, etching sharp shadows which darted in endless motion beneath their eyes. Emily's questionings were clear-cut and bright as the glancing lights and shadows, and Stephen found keen enjoyment in defending and explaining to her quick perception his own and his favorite author's positions, while needle and scythe were alike forgotten.

In the parlor, where the work seemed now to grow tiresome, and the conversation dull, Lina Barry looked in vain from the window and wondered why the mower had so suddenly vanished, and whether he would not return. She had not seen Emily Merle when she came up the walk, nor heard her voice. Emily Merle was the daughter of a clergyman who had been pastor of the Thornton Church for years, and who had now retired from the active work of the ministry by reason of bodily infirmity. They lived in a brick mansion, rich with ivy, on an estate just out of the village which had been Mrs. Merle's inheritance. As Emily was the only child, her education had been the constant study of her parents, and she had, under her father's teaching, become a fine scholar in classic as well as in modern studies. Her vigorous intellect and comprehension, however, were united to a peculiarly sympathetic nature, and thus her culture and position never became a barrier between her and the people among whom she lived. She mingled freely with them with no sense of superiority; in every home, however humble, in Thornton she was a welcome guest.

Stephen Castle, coming to the place as a stranger, had found in Emily Merle an invaluable ally. Clear and impartial in her perceptions, she was able to give the young pastor a co-operation which he could find nowhere else. They had become close friends and fellow-workers, but the relation between them was of frank comradeship, untouched, apparently, by sentiment.

III.

> I watch thy grace; and in its place
>   My heart a charm'd slumber keeps,
> While I muse upon thy face,
>   And a languid fire creeps
>   Thro' my veins to all my frame,
>   Dissolvingly and slowly.
>
> TENNYSON.

"GUESS there's goin' to be a good turnout to-day." It was Mrs. Wescott, better known in Thornton as "Lecty," who spoke in a loud whisper, turning at right angles in her pew to speak to Mrs. Barry in the seat behind her.

It was the first Sunday in July, a few weeks after Mrs. Castle's quilting party, and nearly time for the morning service to begin. The interior of the little church was bare and dull, but it was scrupulously clean, and the dark-green blinds, closed behind the tall, uncolored windows, softened the light, while they permitted spots and bars of sunshine to strike through here and there. Behind the pulpit on the gray wall a group of fluted pillars was painted in fresco, the painter intending to convey to the congregation the illusion that an alcove extended backward at that point; but the perspective was such that no child was ever known to be deceived. Counting and comparing those painted pillars, however, was the prime employment of the Thornton children of tender years during the hours of service, and they thus served a purpose, if not that entertained by their designer. There was a black haircloth sofa in front of the pillars; behind the mahogany pulpit and at one side stood a small unsteady table, on which this morning had been placed a painted glass vase of "hundred-leaf" roses. At the opposite end of the church, in a high gallery, behind a railing and a green curtain, were the singers' seats and the organ.

The congregation did not increase rapidly, nor even very perceptibly, but one after another small groups of women and children and young girls came quietly in and took their seats, while at intervals, after each group, a sunburned man or boy would slip into the end of the pew beside his "women folks," having disposed of his horses, and had his Sunday morning chat with his neighbors under the meeting-house sheds.

The young girls were in most cases dressed in white, with a liberal use of blue and pink ribbons. Their faces wore a look of shyness, amounting nearly to an absence of expression. The older women occasionally smiled and nodded to those who sat near them, and a few were chatting in whispers, but there was, on the whole, a sober silence throughout the room. On the table below the pulpit a bar of sunlight touched to an almost mystic splendor the silver vessels and the snow-white linen of the communion feast which was this morning spread before the people. Seeing this, a more impressible person here and there sat with head slightly bent, but the greater part abstained from even this degree of expression. Emily Merle, in a shaded corner, had bowed her head upon her hand as soon as she took her seat, the simple, restrained expressiveness of her attitude suggesting a quality of devotion rarely high and pure. Her father, a white-haired, venerable man, sat beside her with closed eyes and with a devout expression upon his face.

Meanwhile, as the congregation gradually increased, Lecty continued her whispered observations, saying now : —

"Hayin's over and harvestin' hain't begun

yet, and there is n't anything to keep folks from comin' to meetin' if they wanted to."

"That's so," returned Mrs. Barry; "by next Sunday the men 'll say the horses have got to rest. The wheat's ripe already down in our south lot, and Amasa says he shall begin cuttin' there to-morrow mornin', and after that, you know, there won't be much let-up, not till the wheat's all in." Then, suddenly interrupting herself, she touched Lecty's hand, which hung over the back of the seat, and which held a sprig of fennel, and whispered with lively interest, "Say, Lec, who's that?"

Both women were looking now at a small company of people who were passing up the central aisle — a man and two ladies, one of whom was leading a child.

"Why, that's Lorenzo Deering," whispered Lecty promptly, "and that's his wife, her with the young one. She's a second wife; his first wife was a Cutter, don't you remember? They live in that big brown house on the pike, most to Pembroke, and they don't very often go anywheres to meetin', I guess, but I've seen him here once or twice evenin's this spring. Guess he likes to hear Elder Castle preach."

It was the young lady who was most intently observed.

A Minister of the World

"But who is with them, that other one?" questioned Mrs. Barry.

"I don't know," Lecty confessed reluctantly, adding, "Hush! there's the minister!"

The small organ was piping shrilly as Stephen Castle walked up the aisle, ascended the platform and seated himself behind the pulpit. Every eye was upon him, and a sudden hush seemed to fall upon the people as he bowed his head and so sat before them in silent prayer. However boyish and merry he might be in his every-day mood, however free and accessible in his ministrations to the Thornton people as their pastor, Stephen Castle was always regarded by them with reverence, as one distinctly above and beyond themselves. To hold ordinary conversation with him on the Sabbath day was never thought of. It was his habit to spend the early hours of the day alone in his study, from which he came into the pulpit with a high and solemn aspect, as of one who had seen that which is invisible. Most marked was his rapt and self-forgetting look at the communion season, when he seemed in a peculiar degree to feel the weight of desire for the souls intrusted to him, and all the people, seeing him, felt, if they did not speak it, " He has been praying for us."

The choir now led the people in the Doxology, Lina Barry's sweet, almost childish voice, floating clear and high above them all from her place in the gallery. Standing thus, with Stephen Castle across the church in his place in the pulpit, Lina's blue eyes were fixed on him, and she was suddenly aware of a slight change, a shade of surprise which quickly passed over his face, leaving it quiet as before, but which made Lina look where he had looked — into the pew where the strangers sat, whose coming had been a matter of curiosity and interest to all the congregation, as well as to Lecty and Mrs. Barry.

The service proceeded with prayer and reading, and the whole-souled, honest attempt to sing unto the Lord, which makes the music in a country church often half pathetic. Not a second time did Stephen Castle's glance linger in the spot where the Deerings sat, but wherever he turned his eyes that morning he saw the one face whose look haunted him against his will. Among all those honest, homely faces, with their inflexible reticence, their brief range of expression, their honest but unresponsive attentiveness, his consciousness was thrilled and stirred by the sight of a face so subtly, so marvellously different. He did not know that the face was very beautiful, he only knew the strange, new sense of harmony that it gave him, like a perfect chord of music; neither did he understand the complexities and refinements of feeling and perception which gave that face its play of radiant expression, its swift changes and flashes of light and shade. He only knew that every other face before him suddenly became hard and immobile, as if of wood or stone. Even Emily Merle's seemed strangely dull to him, and Lina Barry's blue eyes were as expressionless as the eyes of a statue.

All this Stephen felt rather than thought, in a succession of impressions which in persons of susceptible imagination make much of the stuff of the mental life. Unconsciously to himself he was stimulated by the presence of that face before him as by new wine, and even those who were most ardent in their admiration of their pastor confessed to each other at the end of the service that they "never saw Elder Castle so much engaged as he was this morning."

When the congregation broke up Stephen, contrary to his custom, remained for a few minutes in the pulpit. He knew if he mingled,

A Minister of the World

as usual, with the people that he must greet Mr. Deering, whom he had met before, and must meet the face of that stranger; and this, for some reason, he feared to do.

Strangers were rarely seen in the little church at Thornton, and the people stood aside and watched with half-averted but observant eyes the two ladies who followed Mr. Deering down the aisle and out from the church to the horse-block, where a man was sitting in a handsome covered carriage holding a pair of well-groomed horses. Young Mrs. Deering and her child received their share of attention, especially from the young mothers who were interested in the dainty gown of the little girl. It was the young lady who accompanied Mrs. Deering, however, who was most intently observed, and there were some who, seeing her that morning and never seeing her again, could still, years after, recall the grace of her slender figure, the exquisite color and texture of her gown, the faint fragrance that passed by with her, and the brilliant light of her smile.

Mrs. Barry, upon whom none of these things were lost, turned back as the door shut upon the stranger, and looked at Lina, who had just come down from the gallery and was standing, in her thick white cotton gown and pink ribbons, with something of disapproval in her eyes. She was a pretty girl, everybody said so, and she had a nice, fair skin, but nothing would ever make her look like that, even her mother was admitting. It was just then that Emily Merle came by with an armful of library books, for it was time for the session of the Sunday-school to open now, and with her clear, untroubled voice said, —

"What a beautiful woman that was, Mrs. Barry! It was a pleasure to look at her."

To which Mrs. Barry replied with a shade of coldness, —

"Why, do you think so? I should never have thought of calling her beautiful, — she was so dark."

Emily Merle made no reply.

IV.

> All may of thee partake;
> Nothing can be so mean,
> Which with this tincture (for thy sake)
> Will not grow bright and clean.
>
> This is the famous stone
> That turneth all to gold;
> For that which God doth touch and own
> Cannot for less be told.
>
> GEORGE HERBERT.

ON the Wednesday following, Stephen Castle was driving his bay mare Doll, between nine and ten in the morning, along the turnpike road, or the old stage road as it was often called, between Thornton and Pembroke. Beside him in his single carriage sat Mrs. Castle in her best gown, with a look of lively but restrained interest on her face.

The morning was breathless with heat already, and the dust from their wheels settled heavily upon the tangled weeds and brambles by the roadside. The pine and spruce trees exhaled a pungent fragrance under the keen July sun, and on the more distant hills shaded to almost a bluish black in its early light. It was midsummer day.

"It's going to be a pretty hot day for a wedding, Stephen. Look how Doll feels the heat already," remarked Mrs. Castle.

"The warmest day yet, I think," Stephen replied in a tone which said plainly that the weather did not interest him vividly. His face wore an abstracted expression, which his mother perceived, and so kept silence for some moments. Whether it was the close sympathy between them which made the same thoughts common to both without words, or whether it was accident, when Mrs. Castle spoke again she touched the subject of Stephen's innermost thought.

"I wonder," she said, after they had driven a mile in silence, "whether the Deerings won't most likely come to Sarah's wedding? I should most think they would, George Allen being their tenant for so many years. What do you think?"

"Very likely they may be there," Stephen replied; and again they rode on in silence until they came in sight of a low, brown farmhouse near the road, with an orchard on one side and a smooth, green yard on the other, sloping down to a vegetable garden. Contrary to custom, the front door of the house was in use to-day and stood open, showing that an event of importance was to take place; and accordingly Stephen drove up to the front steps, instead of to the kitchen door, as was his habit when making pastoral calls. George Allen, the father of the girl whose wedding day it was, stood in his shirt-sleeves ready to greet them and to take the horse around to the barn, and Stephen, after a moment's delay, followed his mother into the house. The small entry had a close smell of new oilcloth, and contained no furniture beyond an oblong, leaved table covered by a red and black printed cloth. On the table stood a crimson fuchsia in full blossom.

Stephen laid his straw hat on the table and went into the square room at the left, called the parlor, which was full of heavy odors of flowers, and closely shut and shaded as if for a funeral. The room was of moderate size, and contained, besides a few chairs and tables, a new melodeon and a polished sheet-iron stove, which was freely decorated with branches of asparagus. The carpet was in violently contrasting shades of red and green, and felt rough and uneven to the feet by reason of its underlining of hay.

A Minister of the World

When Stephen entered the room, there were ten or twelve women standing about its outside limits, with all of whom he shook hands, and then, withdrawing to a corner behind a small table, he stood silent, a small, morocco-bound book in one hand. His look and attitude plainly indicated his disinclination to the small talk with which the women were trying to fill up the time of waiting, and respecting his wishes and standing in especial awe of him as probably passing through mysterious mental conditions appropriate to the discharge of high official function, they left him to himself.

Very soon there was a flutter in the little entry, and Mrs. Allen, in a tidy gown with a little lace about her throat and a bit of pink geranium in her bosom, ushered into the parlor Mr. and Mrs. Deering, accompanied by the lady who had been with them at church on Sunday morning. At the door Mr. Deering was pausing to introduce his wife's friend to Mrs. Allen, with a laughing apology for bringing a stranger to Miss Sarah's wedding.

"Miss Loring" (Stephen heard her name called) "from New York." He heard her voice, and saw her smile and move across the room, as he stood apparently indifferent to all that passed, not lifting his eyelids nor changing his posture, except to fold his arms across his chest, with the little book still in his hand.

The moments passed. The men who had accompanied their wives from distant farms showed a marked disinclination to appear in the parlor, and persistently clung to the refuge of some apple-trees near the barn, biting bits of grass and uneasily trying to be at ease. For a length of time, which began to grow appalling, it seemed almost certain that these wedding guests would not consent to witness the ceremony; and great was the anxiety of their wives, who now confided to each other, with little bursts of nervous laughter, that "the men were always just so," and that "it would serve them right if they got left altogether."

One by one, however, with no evidence of haste, but with an air of reluctance well calculated to deceive a denizen of the outer world, the husbands dropped into the parlor, and stood with their heavy brown hands variously but always uneasily disposed, and their roughened heads bent at different angles.

The situation became more and more awkward; and Stephen Castle, as he stood apart, frowned and bit his lip in the vexation of it, for still the bridal party tarried. Twenty-five people were now standing together under circumstances which hardly admitted of conversation, and where every one felt, none the less, that complete silence was the one calamity which might not be endured. The moments passed painfully. The time before the men had joined the company now seemed incredibly distant and remote, and each woman in her heart justified her husband's superior wisdom which had made him delay in yielding himself a captive to these four walls before the time.

Mrs. Castle, imbued with the idea that it was her duty, as she would have said herself, " to sow beside all waters," could now be heard distinctly in the growing stillness addressing a pale little woman in black who stood nearest her in phrases which, although conversational, were obviously didactic; and death and the grave were frequently mentioned, to the dismay of Miss Loring, who stood in the shelter of the melodeon only a few feet distant.

"Why should he have been taken?" Mrs. Castle was now asking gently but quite firmly of her neighbor, " I asked my husband as we rode home from the grave." The little woman murmured an inarticulate but appreciative response, and at that moment a woman who stood at the other end of the melodeon from Miss Loring was heard to say with cheerful emphasis that she "didn't know whether that child would live to outgrow them fits or not."

Miss Loring felt a wild desire to scream at the top of her voice, but restrained herself; and Mrs. Castle could now be heard leading her submissive hearer up through successive stages of resignation to a position which seemed to imply a decided preference that Stephen's infant brother had been taken out of this present evil world. Anything from her after this would have been an anti-climax. Plainly this line of argument ought to have lasted until the appearance of the bridal party; but still they did not come, although the ceremony had been appointed for ten o'clock, and it was already ten minutes later. No one dared now to speak for fear of being in the midst of an inappropriate sentence when the eventful moment should come, and every one in the room was occupied with avoiding the eye of every other person, — the men on general principles, the women for fear they should be betrayed into hysterical laughter, — when suddenly a broad-shouldered, sunburned young fellow, with a rosy-cheeked girl on his arm, in a light gray gown and neatly braided hair, appeared in the doorway, and stepped rather rapidly across the room to the appointed corner where Stephen Castle had been standing so long.

Looking with searching directness into their anxious young faces, Stephen spoke; and instantly all the nervous tension of the moment, all its grotesque blending of the funereal with the festive quality, was dispelled. His voice was full and deep, and vibrated with a tender authority which seemed to transform those two commonplace-looking persons into children of God exalted by His grace to highest privilege. The room became a sacred place, and those two were brought face to face with God. When the final words of blessing were spoken, Miss Loring, lifting her eyes and seeing the white, strained face of the girl's mother as she turned to her child, and the emotion on the two young faces, could not restrain her tears, and they were still wet upon her lashes when some one beside her spoke a word of introduction, and Stephen Castle, with the seriousness of his office still upon him, took her hand and spoke to her with grave courtesy.

V.

> The encounter of the wise, —
> Say, what other metre is it
> Than the meeting of the eyes?
> Nature poureth into Nature
> Through the channels of that feature,
> Riding on the ray of sight,
> Fleeter far than whirlwinds go,
> Or for service or delight,
> Hearts to hearts their meaning show,
> Sum their long experience,
> And impart intelligence.
> Single look has drained the breast,
> Single moment years confessed.
> EMERSON.

JUST how it happened Stephen did not clearly understand at the time, although afterward it became sufficiently plain to him, but a few minutes later he found himself standing in the green seclusion of the old orchard at the north side of the farmhouse, leaning against a stout-limbed apple-tree, while Miss Loring sat before him in a hammock, which had been stretched there by the young people whom they had just left in the close parlor.

"How good it is to be in the air," she said gently.

Stephen nodded without speaking. He was stirred by the emotions of the last half-hour, and confused by his nearness to this beautiful woman. He recognized fully now that she was beautiful, with her gray eyes under long dark lashes, her face set like a flower upon the round white throat, and the wonderful ripple and glint of her bright brown hair, which curled off delicately from her temples. There was something in the contour of her head and in the poise of it which vaguely recalled to him classic heads of fair Greek women. Her throat was bare to a point below its soft white hollow, and the round arms from the elbow down. Stephen had never seen women who wore their gowns in this fashion, and it gave him a shamefaced unwillingness to look at her. She was dressed in cream-white stuff, thin and soft, with lines of yellow in it here and there, but without frills or furbelows, and she wore no jewels. The outline of her head and waist, as she sat in the hammock, was girlish; and yet Stephen was sure that she was not very young, perhaps not younger than himself.

As he did not speak, she began again; this

time her look seemed to compel him to lift his eyes and to meet hers.

"I must tell you," she said timidly, "how very wonderful it was, what you did there in that marriage ceremony. I never felt myself in such an absurd position in my life; it all seemed perfectly droll and dreadful to me at the beginning. I was wondering if they were going to bring in a dead person every minute, all the talk was so grewsome and dismal; and when that poor frightened fellow appeared with his great hands in those ghastly white gloves, it was worse than ever. I felt as if I should disgrace myself by some outburst; but the moment you spoke the situation was completely altered, redeemed, don't you know? It all became noble and beautiful, and I never in my life felt what such things meant as I did while you were speaking. Please do not mind my telling you; I almost felt that I ought, you see."

She spoke beseechingly, for Stephen had lowered his eyes again; her words seemed to beat them down, and his face was very grave. A strange tumult was going on within the young man's mind, awakened by her words not less than by her presence. He saw the scene they had left through her eyes suddenly, as he could never have seen it before, in all its grotesqueness, and he was angry with her for making him see it, angry that his world was so far apart from hers. Closely mingled with this feeling was a strange, exciting perception that in the real nature of things it was to her world that he belonged. Her grace and charm, her subtle sympathy, her swift perception of the good in what he said, were what he craved, were what belonged to him. No one else had ever given all this to him. Emily Merle was bright and clear-headed, and she was his good comrade, but she never hesitated to point out his mistakes, and criticise his opinions. He thought of her now for an instant, with a faint sense of indignation, as he raised his eyes at last, and by an odd little accident caught sight of a name embroidered in delicate tracery on the handkerchief which lay in Miss Loring's lap. Then all thought of Emily was forgotten in the surprise with which he read the name, "Stephanie." It was a new name to him. How strange that her name should be the counterpart of his own! Was there not a meaning in it? A sudden flash of intelligence passed between their eyes as his were lifted from the handkerchief, and Stephen colored deeply.

"I wonder if you know that my name is Stephen," he said simply.

"Yes," she returned; "how very strange it is. We ought to be good friends. There ought to be, do you not think so, a kind of invisible affinity between us?"

"I believe there is," Stephen answered soberly, seeking to hide a strange, intoxicating sense of exultation which seemed mounting hotly to his brain.

And yet, as he followed Stephanie Loring under the orchard boughs into the farmhouse, whither they were now called to the wedding feast, there was beneath the excitement of the moment a perception, not fully clear as yet to his own consciousness, that it was less to her that he owed this affinity of which they had spoken than to what she stood for, — the unknown world of beauty and art and human perfection to which she belonged.

In the week which followed the wedding Stephen Castle spent many hours at the Deerings', having been invited to call by Mrs. Deering when they met after the marriage. He found great enjoyment in the hospitable house, where he was welcomed with unfeigned cordiality whenever he presented himself, and given the freedom of the pleasant rooms and grounds.

Stephanie Loring remained with the Deerings throughout another week, and Stephen always found himself her guest in particular. She played and sang to him as he sat in the great music-room, and opened to his possession a new realm, for he had never until now heard good music. At other times they sat under the oak-trees near the house; and while she was busy with some dainty handiwork, he read aloud from books which he loved, and which she received with quick insight and responsive sympathy.

Then there were long, quiet talks in the evenings on the piazza, which some way always turned at last upon the church to which Stephanie belonged in New York: how it was without a pastor; how sadly it needed just the right man; how she wished — but here she always interrupted herself or was interrupted by Stephen.

Stephen would drive home in the darkness or in the starlight after these long visits, which for the time absorbed his days, with his thoughts in a riot. What was coming to him? Could it be that he did not belong, after all, to the Thornton parish and to the people who loved him so tenderly? Was it disloyalty to let his mind dwell on these new possibilities? Surely other men left their churches. Might it not be that another man could reach the hearts of these people better than he? How rarely was a word said to show that his sermons had made even the slightest impression! Stephanie Loring discussed them freely with him; noticed all the fine points, the impressive passages; and Stephen found her appreciation very sweet. How would it be to live among people like her, — quick to perceive his best, gracious and delicate in their recognition of his work? How would it be to be in a position of influence, — not to be a country pastor any more? What would the fellows say if such a thing ever did happen? What would Dr. Endicott of the Divinity School say? Stephen had always felt, with a mingled humility and resentment, that the old Doctor did not rate his ability very high. It would not be altogether distasteful to him to make the Doctor open his eyes! Thus his thoughts, earnest or idle, would cross each other in endless motion like waves of the sea, as he drove along the silent roads, through the sweetness of the clover-fields wet with dew.

A Minister of the World

But it often happened that when he turned down the hill above the little white church, and saw it lying there under the quiet sky, with the parsonage in the grassy yard beyond, all these thoughts would yield to a yearning tenderness for the simple place, and the simple people who so faithfully loved him and so patiently allowed themselves to be led by him.

When August came, the excitement was over; for Stephanie Loring, having prolonged her visit to her old friend far beyond its first limits, had taken her departure to join her family at Newport for the remainder of the season. When she parted from Stephen, she had looked straight into his eyes, and had said significantly:

"I shall see you again. This is not where you belong, but I must not say any more. You will understand."

VI.

> Deep in the man sits fast his fate
> To mould his fortunes mean or great;
> Unknown to Cromwell as to me
> Was Cromwell's measure or degree.
>
> EMERSON.

STEPHEN went back from the charmed life he had been leading to the uneventful days in the parsonage with his mother, and to his intercourse with the farmers and their families. He was not the same, and, with honest pain in his heart, he saw that he could never be the same again. He felt a weariness and distaste for the people about him. And yet he strove earnestly to come back into harmony with his people and his work, and sometimes he fancied he was succeeding.

It was Emily Merle who showed him that this was a delusion, as he strolled home with her from the Wednesday evening prayer-meeting.

"Do you want me to tell your fortune, Mr. Castle?" she asked, half laughingly, half sadly.

"Yes, Emily; I wish somebody was wise enough to do it. It is very dim to me just now."

"That is because you are in the confusion of a great change coming, I think," she said in a voice which was cheerful but not steady. "That lovely lady at the Deerings' was a new star in your sky, and she is bringing great changes to you, and in you as well. Perhaps others do not see it, but it is quite clear to me."

"How do you mean? I do not understand," Stephen protested uneasily.

"You are not for us any more. You are for her, and she will draw you to her."

"Do you mean that I love her, Emily?" Stephen spoke abruptly, as if it were a relief to him to touch the subject.

"I do not know," Emily replied. "There is no reason why you should not. I know she must attract you strongly, and that she will influence your life always. Perhaps you love her, I cannot tell."

"She is like a wonderful new book to me," Stephen confessed. "She fascinates me, and yet she does not touch my heart. She is too fine for me, Emily. She would never look at a country boy like me. You are my best friend, my sister in a way, dear Emily. I can talk to you even of this."

"I wonder if you know how changed you have become since Miss Loring came here?" Emily continued. "You are tired of us all; our ways and our doings are stale, flat, and unprofitable. Sometimes I think I understand just how dull and dreary it seems; we all say the things we have always said in meeting, and no one is bright and clever like Miss Loring. I saw how you felt to-night when Mrs. Wescott said she 'felt like settin' her stakes and startin' out anew,' and when Jacob Poole said, as he always does, that he knew he 'was n't anything but a poor failable worm of the dust.'"

"What did you see?" asked Stephen, surprised.

"How all these things, which you used to smile over a little, but in a tender kind of way, as the poor attempts of those whom you truly cared for, vex you now; make you impatient even, I think; give you a feeling of humiliation that the people to whom you belong are so rude and uneducated, and all that."

Stephen did not reply. With her usual clear vision Emily had seen into his innermost thought. He was ashamed, but he was too honest to deny the truth of what she said.

After a short silence — they had reached her gate by this time — Emily said in a voice which was quite steady now, —

"When you go away, for you will before very long, — you know I have the gift of second sight sometimes, — I shall be glad in a certain way for you, Mr. Castle."

"Call me Stephen, if you will, Emily," he interrupted her gently, "when we are by ourselves, at least."

With no touch of coquetry Emily accepted the suggestion in a quiet, natural way, and went on:

"As I was saying, I shall be glad, Stephen, although the difference to us here in Thornton will be very hard to bear. But the change for you is simply in the natural order for a man of your gifts and tastes. I should think the only thing to fear might be that gifts and tastes would, perhaps, rule the day in the new life, not the old convictions and motives, — those, you know, which make all souls of equal worth to us, as I suppose they must be before God."

Emily faltered a little, and spoke timidly. But he had scarcely noticed her last words, so surprised was he with the manner in which she took it for granted that he was to leave Thornton.

They parted a moment later, and Stephen sat for hours in his study that evening pondering upon all these things, and also upon a letter from Stephanie Loring which the evening mail had brought him, and which had kept her before him all through the meeting by its faint suggestion of the odor of violets.

September and October passed quietly in Thornton, with no events beyond those common to the place and people. The harvests were gathered, the leaves fell and huddled in heaps at the edges of the woods, the fields lay in dull, rich tones of green and russet, and the farmers began to have time to look about them a little and to make ready for the long winter.

Lina Barry was now known to be " going with " a prosperous young man whose father's farm adjoined that of her father, and for whom she had been set apart by tacit consent since her childhood, until the advent of Stephen Castle had suddenly given a spur to her mother's ambition, and stirred a romantic interest in the girl's heart. For a time she had treated her old lover coldly, influenced more by her mother's wishes than her own; but of late she had been more favorably inclined to him, and Mrs. Wescott, as usual, gave voice to the

A Minister of the World

popular feeling in Thornton when she said that "for her part she was glad Mis' Barry had got through settin' poor Liny's cap at Elder Castle. 'T wa'n't no kind o' use, if she did beat the county on doughnuts."

Stephen Castle, observing what had come to pass, although he never suspected, being a modest fellow, that Lina had felt more than an ordinary interest in himself, recalled, as if it had been a dream of the night, unreal and impossible, a time when Lina had seemed to him the ideal wife for some man, even fancying himself the man. His mother, who had hoped for such an event, began now to feel the change in him, and grew uneasy and depressed; but she kept her thoughts to herself with inborn reserve.

It was in November, one Sunday morning, that something happened which shook Thornton throughout its length and breadth. This bombshell consisted merely in the presence of two strange gentlemen at the morning service. They came late and left early, driving out from Pembroke, and they made themselves known to no one. Mrs. Wescott, who sat behind them during the service, however, formed her own conclusions, which she imparted to a knot of women in a corner of the vestry at noon.

"They set right in front of me," she said, "and they was both dressed in their black broadcloth, as fine as satin, and their collars and cuffs shone so you could 'most see your face in them. One of them had on a big ring with a stone in it; he was the young one. The old feller, he had the long, gray side whiskers, and looked kind o' militerry. And now let me jest tell you that as sure 's my name 's Electy Wescott and I 'm standin' here, that man was own father to that han'some-lookin' young woman that come here to church a couple of times with the Deerings. Don't you remember? He had jest such eyes, and jest such a way of holdin' his head. And if you want to know what I felt like callin' out when I see them two men stealin' out of the church, I 'll tell you: 'Shoot them while they 're goin' through the door! They 've come here to steal our minister.'"

"But what makes you think so, Lec?" somebody asked.

"Think so? I know so," Lecty sniffed contemptuously. "Those men don't hail from Pembroke, and they don't hail from anywheres this side of the city of New York. Now that much I 'll bet you, if it is Sunday, and in the meetin'-house too! What did they come up here in their broadcloth and gold rings for, and come out to Thornton to meetin' if 't wa'n't jest to spy out what kind of a preacher we'd got? Oh, yes, I've heard of sech things before now. That's the way they do it in them big city churches. They hear that some poor little strugglin' church in the country has got a minister they love and they're all united on, and they think, 'Well, if he's as smart as they say, maybe he'll do for us; he's most likely too big a man for country folks.' But they don't send and ask him to come and preach a sermon to them fair and square. No, they send a couple of spies to see if they think he'll do, and then they wait a spell, and the next thing you know your minister's got took sudden to go off and pay a visit to his old pastor, or to his grandmother, or else it's to look at a new organ. He keeps kind o' still about what direction he's goin' to travel in, but pretty soon he gets a call and then, 'Hurrah, boys! It's off and away to the city.' It's the Lord callin' and no mistake! You'll see if it don't come out as I say."

And so it did, in fact, befall. A month from that day Stephen Castle read his resignation as pastor of the Thornton church, in order to accept the call of the Church of All Good Spirits in New York City to become their pastor. He spoke in frank and manly fashion to his people, who heard him with blinding tears. He told them plainly that he had become restless and dissatisfied, not through any fault of theirs, but because he wanted to be where he could improve and develop among other men. He expected life to be harder than it had been here, where they had all been so gentle to his faults and mistakes, and he knew that he could never love any other people as he loved them.

"All the same he's goin'," said Mrs. Wescott at the close of the service, mopping her eyes with a very wet handkerchief. "And I don't see any kind o' use, for my part, in gettin' a new bonnet this winter, do you, Aunt Elizy?"

The old lady sat beside her in the pew, and a tear was slipping quietly down her withered cheek.

"That's your way of putting it, Electy," she said quietly. "There don't seem very much left to live for, not just now. But it's all right, Stephen," she said, looking up into the face of the young man, who had come to the end of the pew and stood leaning over to speak to

A Minister of the World

her with flushed face and dim eyes. "It's all right, Stephen. It will be a different life from this for you, and you're young and strong, and you ought to have a chance to grow. I'm sorry for the people here. I sha'n't stay long to mind it. I expected you would be close by when the call came for me, and I thought I should like to have you hold my hand; but it's all right." And the little old lady looked up through her tears in the bright, sweet way which Stephen loved.

"You are to send for me when you want me, Aunt Eliza," he said earnestly, his own voice breaking. "I will come to you. I promise to. I shall never change to my Thornton people; they will always be mine, just as much as they are now," he was protesting; but she put up her finger and lightly touched his lips, and said with a quaint smile, —

"You think so now, but you will know better when you are older."

VII.

> The sole thing that I remark
> About the difficulty, this:
> We do not see it where it is,
> At the beginning of the race;
> As we proceed, it shifts its place,
> And where we looked for crowns to fall,
> We find the tug's to come, — that's all.
>
> BROWNING.

"STEPHEN, did you say that Mr. Wells was a deacon of your church?"

It was Mrs. Castle who spoke, leaning back in a cushioned armchair in a tiny and much-upholstered reception-room. It was one of a small suite of furnished rooms which they had taken in an apartment house in New York. It was night, and twelve o'clock by the French clock on the mantel, which told the hour in a tone far more melodious than that of the old timepiece which presided over the parsonage living-room in Thornton.

The face of this was encircled by the arms of certain smiling and gilded nymphs, of whose general effect Mrs. Castle strongly disapproved. She felt uneasily that they expressed the tendency, which prevailed in her new environment, to diminish the emphasis on the solemn passing of the hours, — the view of life as "a winter's day, a journey to the tomb." Feeling this now with peculiar distinctness, she listened severely to the silvery softness of the tone with which the hour was told.

Mrs. Castle wore a new black silk gown which she had had made in Pembroke before leaving Thornton two weeks ago, and it sat primly on her narrow, stiffened form. She wore black kid gloves over her work-hardened hands, through which the enlarged joints would show themselves, and she carried stiffly in one hand a starched handkerchief precisely folded. Her face was pale, and wore a disturbed and anxious expression. They had just returned in Mr. Loring's carriage from a reception given in Stephen's honor at that gentleman's house. There had been an official reception to the new pastor at the chapel of the Church of All Good Spirits the week before. The affair of this evening had been purely social, although it was within its purpose to enable the members of the church, or rather those belonging to the inner circle, to become better acquainted with Stephen Castle.

In reply to his mother's question, Stephen, who had thrown himself upon a divan and was looking intently at the pink and green frescos on the ceiling over his head, remarked, in a slightly defensive tone, —

"Certainly, mother. Why do you ask the question in such a way?"

"It don't seem possible," Mrs. Castle returned, with something between a groan and a sigh. "I guess Christians in New York are n't much like Christians out in the country, or churches, or deacons."

"In some outward points I suppose they are different," said Stephen, kindly; "but at heart I have no doubt they are alike everywhere."

"Well, I don't know, Stephen. It looks very queer to me, and I guess I sha'n't ever feel at home very much in your new church. This Mr. Wells, and you say he's a deacon, stood right beside my chair there, a spell before they dished their icecream, and he was talking to a young man about a whist-party — that's what he called it — that was going to be at his house — I mean Mr. Wells's house — and he was urging that young man, Stephen, to come there and play cards! And he's a deacon in your church! It must be a different kind of

A Minister of the World

a church to any I ever was acquainted with, where the deacons themselves play cards and entice young men into such sinful pleasures, as if they would n't go fast enough themselves. I don't know, I never felt so in my life. It seemed as if it kind of struck to my stomach;" and Mrs. Castle, who had sat up with sudden energy as she talked, dropped her head again on the back of the chair.

As Stephen said nothing, she soon began again, —

"That was n't the only thing, nor the worst thing. How did you feel when you saw those women, — the way they were dressed? Did you think a minister of the Gospel belonged in such a place?" and a flush came in her faded cheeks, and an indignant spark in her eyes.

"Don't get so stirred up, mother," Stephen said soothingly. "You must remember that we are not used to city ways yet."

"No, and I thank the Lord I am not used to city ways, if those are city ways, and I pray I never shall be! I was all mixed up one time," she continued, after a little pause, "and I suppose some of the folks had a laugh at my ignorance; but I guess it's just as well not to know too much about some things. One of those pretty-looking young girls that wore so much of that thin gauzy stuff come up to me, and got an introduction and talked a little. She looked pleasant enough, but she hadn't much to say, and I hadn't, and I was just hoping you would come around and propose to go home, when she said, 'Have you seen Miss Owen yet?' and I said, 'No, I don't think she's been introduced, though she may have been; it's hard remembering so many names.' At that I saw she looked kind of puzzled, and then she said, 'Oh, I don't mean anybody here, I was speaking of Miss Marie Owen who has been playing Juliet at the Metropolitan. You must be sure to go and see her.'"

Stephen could not restrain a smile at this, knowing that his mother had always regarded a theatre as having geographically a close proximity to the realms of darkness.

"What did you say?" he asked.

"Say? What should a Christian say? I said, 'No, my dear, I shall never be seen inside of a theatre while I have my senses, and I want to ask you if you think it is a place for an immortal soul on its way to eternity to be found? How would you like to be called to die in such a place?' When I put it straight to her conscience, I could see it went home; she colored up, and said she was sorry she had made such a mistake. Then I told her I was sorry too, but the gates of mercy was wide open even for those that had wandered far. It was just then that you came up, and I left her."

There was a little silence in the room. Stephen was looking at his mother with a pang in his heart, as he saw the keen suffering she was enduring for his sake. She had been very silent since they reached New York, although there had been a homeless, piteous look upon her face as she moved about the small, over-furnished rooms of their new domicile, — a home they could hardly call it, — vaguely seeking for something to do. The rooms were kept in order for them; she did not even have the privilege of making her own bed, and she was too timid to ask for it, and they took their meals in the general dining-room of the house. But all the bitter homesickness in her heart Mrs. Castle would have kept resolutely to herself. Stephen had felt it his duty to respond to the call to this new church, and she would follow, cost what it might. But now her conscience had been alarmed; an awful fear had overtaken her that the Church of All Good Spirits was not the Church of God, and she could keep silence no longer.

Stephen Castle was not a small man. Some men in his position would have been mortified by the display of rustic ignorance on the part of his mother, and would have yielded to the irritation which such a feeling would incite. But the young man was too profoundly affected himself to give way to petty or superficial considerations. He had made like discoveries which amazed and shocked him no less than they had his mother, and in his own heart he was simply appalled at the situation before him. These two people had lived all their lives in remote, inland villages of Northern New England. The most rigid Puritanic scruples had been handed down through successive generations. It had been a ministerial family, characterized hitherto by respectable but not marked ability, and by the most unflinching devotion to a sense of duty. Mrs. Castle was a somewhat narrow woman, but she was the product of generations ready to die at the stake or in battle for the sake of principle, and the same stuff was in her. In her son was a strain of the imaginative, idealizing temperament, — more of flexibility, less of severity. Furthermore, he was bound to be hopeful by all the exigencies of the position.

"Well, mother," he said, rising and opening the door into her room, "we must remember that we have not all the truth ourselves, and we may find much that is good underneath these appearances which trouble us so to-night. Don't lie awake. Don't worry. God will help us, perhaps, to make these people over in some way. Perhaps that is what He brought me here for."

"If they don't make you over into one of their own kind instead, Stephen; that is what I am most afraid of;" and Mrs. Castle looked with piercing keenness into her son's face.

"Hardly," he said, with a faint attempt at a smile. "I have too much of your blood in my veins for that. Good-night!"

VIII.

> Through what tears and sweat and pain
> Must he gain
> Fruitage from the tree of life!
> Shall it yield him bitter flavor?
> Shall its savor
> Be as manna midst the turmoil and the strife?
>
> EMMA LAZARUS.

MR. LORING, the father of Stephanie, was in certain ways the most influential member of the Church of All Good Spirits. He was a man of much wealth and some culture, of great personal popularity, with a decided interest in the affairs of the church; but in this and in all things he was keen, although not unscrupulous, a master at manœuvre, and, first and last and always, a business man. It was thus a matter of no great difficulty for Stephanie to bring about the call to Stephen Castle, which was, as must have been inferred, the immediate result of her efforts. All through the months at Newport she had talked to her father of the wonderfully brilliant young preacher whom she had discovered away off among the New England hills. She had dwelt upon his physical power and beauty, upon his personal charm and magnetism, and upon his intellectual promise, until her father, who was chairman of the pulpit committee of his church, finally consented to present the name of Stephen Castle at the first committee meeting held in October. He did this with easy, laughing apology for calling the attention of the gentlemen to "a country boy," for he supposed him to be really nothing more, but he had heard — how, he omitted to say — that he was a fellow of extraordinary talent, and, of course, other things being equal, nothing would draw like a young enthusiastic man in the pulpit. He would probably be a little green and countrified at first, but that could be depended upon to wear off, etc., etc. As he and Stephanie had expected, Mr. Loring, with another member of the committee, was deputed to go to Thornton quietly and to hear the young man preach. We know the results of this errand.

The negotiations with Stephen himself had impressed the young clergyman as more purely businesslike than he would have wished; but he felt himself at a certain disadvantage with these polished, elegant men, and distrusted his own impressions.

"Your preaching is what we want," Mr. Loring had said. "Pastoral work is not expected in our church, except in extreme cases, — illness and death. You will, of course, meet our people frequently at dinners and receptions and all that. We shall try to make it pleasant for you socially. But what our church wants is good preaching, — brains, in short, Mr. Castle; and that is what we have secured. We are entirely satisfied on that point. Your salary will be five thousand, — not as large as it ought to be, but perhaps a little advance on what you are having now, — and I think you can live on it, in a quiet way, of course, — a little apartment, you know, or something of that sort. We will try to help you out. My daughter is great on all that kind of thing."

This conversation occurred in New York after the Sunday which Stephen had spent there in the late autumn. He had returned to Thornton and the little parsonage; and as he stepped upon the yellow painted floor of the narrow piazza, passing the now leafless rose-bushes, he thought with a kind of shame that it was this house and eight hundred dollars a year which he was exchanging for a salary of five thousand. The shame was lest it would seem to every one who knew it that it was this difference which had dazzled and drawn him away from Thornton, and in his heart of hearts Stephen Castle knew it was not this. But it was not until weeks afterward that he could bring himself to mention the subject of his salary, even to his mother.

In the plans for their new residence, and all their domestic arrangements, Stephanie Loring's help had been of the utmost importance to them. She had shown herself most sincerely interested in caring for Mrs. Castle's comfort. It was to her that Stephen went for light and knowledge on all doubtful points which came up in his new life; and this was precisely what she had expected.

A few days after the reception at Mr. Loring's, Stephen called at the house, the conventional brown-stone front in the correct section of Fifth Avenue, and found Stephanie alone in the library. There was delicate flattery in the gladness with which she greeted him, and he felt an exquisite pleasure in watching her grace and loveliness as she sat near him, and in meeting the radiance of her smile as they exchanged a few gay repartees, an accomplishment which Stephen was learning readily. But he was not in a gay mood at heart, and soon he said with a sudden, impatient gesture, —

"Do you know, Miss Loring, what an awful blunder it was, bringing me here?"

"No, I have not discovered the blunder yet," she rejoined promptly, skilfully hiding her dismay at his words, for she knew that he spoke seriously.

"May I talk with you plainly?" he asked. "I am tired, — not bodily, but in the head and heart of me, — and I want to say things as I really feel them, not as I am expected to say them."

"I wish you would speak perfectly plainly. I want you to with me always," Stephanie said, in a voice which was half caressing in its gentleness.

"Thank you. Well, in the first place, if you will let me say it, All Good Spirits is a fashionable church, an ultra-fashionable church. I have found this out by a little questioning here and there where I was not known; and I find they call it the 'Boudoir Church,' and the 'All Swells' Church,' and all that kind of thing. This is the simple fact. The church is intended for the wealthy and aristocratic class, and for them alone. That is not the kind of church I ever ought to serve. I am country born and bred. More than that, many things which are matters of course in New York fashionable society are simply monstrous to me. The extravagance in flowers and on the table at these dinners and receptions seems to me actually wicked, — you see I am speaking plainly; the way the ladies dress, the way they all amuse themselves! I am perplexed, confused, at a loss utterly. I have always supposed that all these things were what belonged to 'the world' in the Scriptural sense, and that the abstaining from them was essential to the Christian life. But the members of my church practise these things continually, without scruple or restraint. What does it mean? Are they all wrong, or am I all wrong? How can two walk together unless they are agreed?" and Stephen looked into Stephanie's face with unsmiling eyes. His own face was stern and white.

She had flushed when he had begun his talk, but her face was clear now and composed.

"It would hardly be graceful to remind you," she said, smiling, "who it was that said, 'Why was not this ointment sold for three hundred pence and given to the poor?'"

"Yes," he returned quickly, "but it was upon the feet of Christ that the ointment was poured; and all this lavish waste is for personal, even sensuous pleasure, so far as I can see."

"Forgive me, Mr. Castle, but I think you are wrong there. Do you not see that there may be unselfishness in the expenditure of several hundred dollars in the beauty of flowers by a woman who calls her friends together for the sake of giving them happiness? The underlying, perhaps I ought to say the ideal, motive in all our entertaining is to brighten life for one another, to give it joy and charm. Now, I claim that this is a right motive. How much ought to be spent in this way is for each person to judge himself. Perhaps the woman who spent two hundred dollars for her dinner the other night had sent two thousand for the work in the lower part of the city."

"I see the line you are taking, — I am glad you have as good a one. I suppose we all give some place to beauty and enjoyment in our lives."

"To be sure we do. Those people at the wedding where I met you, in Thornton, had washed up their pickle jars and filled them with roses and peonies, and I respected the

A Minister of the World

effort they had made for beauty and festivity. It is a need of nature in all of us, and I can see nothing worse in my sending an order for flowers to my florist where I am trying to make a number of people forget for a little that life is a 'horrid grind.' It helps the florist, it gives pleasure, it cultivates the sense of beauty."

"But how about the amusements? They sit still heavier on my soul."

"There, Mr. Castle, you will have to allow me to say the question is simply one of education. You have been brought up to think it was right to play with dominoes and croquet balls, and wrong to play with cards and billiard balls; right to listen to tame or lame elocution, wrong to witness the magnificent interpretations of men like Booth and Jefferson. Most people in this part of the world think that all these recreations are alike as far as moral quality is concerned, and the question which they shall use is merely one of taste and preference."

"But there are certainly degrading associations with card-playing and the theatre which make them unsuitable for use by thoughtful Christian people."

"So everything about us is capable of abuse. But is it not better to learn self-restraint and the proper proportioning of these things to the earnest work of our lives, than to frown indiscriminately upon bad and good alike? Is it not really a higher use of one's moral perceptions?" and she looked into his face with the witchery of her wonderfully brilliant smile.

"I do not know. I confess you bewilder me. I shall have to go home and quietly analyze what you have said, and see of what it is made. I have a lingering fear that sophistry and self-indulgence are not altogether absent from the position you defend, and yet you have made me see things from your point of view."

He had risen now to go, and she stood facing him before the fireplace.

"And you will not say again that you have made a blunder in coming to us?" she asked, looking wistfully at him, and holding out both her hands.

He took them in his, and looked down into her face, his own much moved.

"It could not be a blunder to come where you led me," he said. "Perhaps — I do not know — I could not choose but follow;" and with that he was gone.

Stephanie, standing alone, as the house door shut, clasped her hands together, and her eyes flashed with a sudden light, unlike the pleading softness which had just now been in them.

"He, too, is a man!" she whispered to herself with something like exultation; "even he, at last, is human!"

IX.

I have stifled more than one nascent love. Why? Because, with that prophetic certainty which belongs to moral intuition, I felt it *lacking in true life, and less durable than myself.* I choked it down in the name of the supreme affection to come. The loves of sense, of imagination, of sentiment, — I have seen through and rejected them all; I sought the love which springs from the central profundities of being. — AMIEL.

NEARLY three years have passed since Stephen Castle became pastor of the Church of All Good Spirits, and on an evening in early spring we find him in a select company at the house of one of his parishioners, Mrs. Petersham. Dinner is over, and the guests are standing in groups about the great drawing-room, which is magnificently furnished, and rich with paintings, bronzes, and porcelains of rare value.

Mrs. Petersham, who is a widow of large wealth, has a son of the age of Stephen Castle, and between the two men a friendship has sprung up. As a result the young pastor had been abroad with the Petershams on a journey of several months in the preceding summer and fall.

To-night Stephen is among the guests, but his old Thornton friends might hesitate a moment before they recognized him. He is in full dress, with a single white rose in his buttonhole, and above the broad white expanse of his shirt front his face rises paler and thinner than they knew it, and its expression, half dreamy and indifferent, would strike them as yet more strangely altered. The old boyish frankness, the eager happiness, has gone from the face, and with it the indescribable spiritual elevation which made it so like the face of some strong young saint. The face is at once prouder and sadder than it used to be, more intellectually refined, more reserved, less earnest.

He was standing now before a painting on an easel in a curtained recess, a gentleman and lady with him. He was leaning against the wall of the alcove, with something of languid grace in his attitude, unlike his old alertness, and with eyelids drawn narrowly he surveyed the picture with critical scrutiny.

"Yes, I saw it in Paris," he replied to the lady who had just asked him a question; "but that was five months ago. Mrs. Petersham has only received it within a day or two."

"It was at the Salon, was it not?"

A Minister of the World

"Yes. It is a wonderful thing." Stephen spoke the last words almost under his breath.

The painting showed a woman, exquisitely beautiful, reclining under green ilex-trees. The landscape was plainly Grecian. Beside her, prone and submissive, lay a tiger. One of her fair white arms was dropped across his sleek, tawny shoulders. Her attitude was of indolent repose, her face dreamily content; only the eyes were fixed with eager desire upon the sea, where a storm-tossed boat could be seen passing near the shore, the sailors looking shoreward with anxious faces.

Across the room Stephanie Loring was the centre of a group where several gentlemen were vying with one another in winning her smiles and attention. She was dressed with unusual elegance, in gleaming white satin, with a fall of lace around her beautiful shoulders; and her brilliant beauty and wit made her the central point of the company.

It was not long before she slipped away from the people she was with, and came quietly into the recess where Stephen Castle was still regarding the picture. He was alone now.

"I must see this wonderful new picture," she said, not looking at Stephen, but standing so near him that the lace of her dress touched his arm. "Mrs. Petersham always finds the loveliest things," she added, in her clear, cool tone *de société*.

For a moment they stood in silence; then Stephanie said in a lower voice, through which some inner feeling vibrated, —

"Do you like it? The subject is always so disagreeable, I think. I wonder that you should find so much in it, Mr. Castle."

"It is a great picture to me," he said, half carelessly; "it is what it suggests, not what it shows, which gives it power."

"Oh, I see," she responded lightly, "it might make good sermon material. Naturally! How stupid I was! I shall expect a famous sermon to young men before long, with Mrs. Petersham's pretty Circe — she is certainly extremely pretty — for a text. I can see how you could use it charmingly."

"Oh, thank you," said Stephen, with mock gratitude.

"But really, Mr. Castle, you do use a classic *motif* like that wonderfully. I heard so many persons speak of the sermon into which you wove the Iphigenia story. It made a very great impression."

A Minister of the World

Just then Lloyd Petersham joined them, announcing that the carriages were ready now and it was time to leave for the opera. Patti was singing in opera. Mrs. Petersham's guests were to occupy her box that evening at the Academy. As Stephen and Stephanie turned to join the others, Lloyd Petersham said, —

"Oh, by the way, Castle, I stopped at your rooms on my way up to-night, thinking you might not have left, and they gave me this letter for you. It was all the afternoon mail brought you, I believe;" and he handed Stephen a letter. It was in a yellow envelope, and the address was written in a stiff, uncertain hand. The postmark was Thornton. Murmuring his thanks, Stephen slipped the letter into his pocket and followed his friend to the dressing-room. He rode in the carriage with Mrs. Petersham to the Academy; and when they entered the box, which was full of flowers and fragrance, Stephen quietly took a chair behind Stephanie, in the background of the gay company, where he could be still if he chose.

They were late; one act was already over, and the violins were sighing in yearning tones over the overture to the second. The curtain rose; the prima-donna sang her bravest; the audience went wild; and then the curtain fell, and the lights flared up again.

It was at this time that Stephen for some reason remembered the letter in his pocket, and turning, to be unobserved, he broke the seal and looked at the signature. He found this to be "Electa Wescott," and immediately he reversed the sheet and read the letter through. It was as follows: —

MR. CASTLE.

DEAR AND REVEREND SIR, — I have the sad news to give you that Aunt Eliza is no more. She had not been sick in bed, but failing slowly, and on Sunday evening, just after the second service, she breathed her last without a struggle. I may truly say that she died in peace. You was one of the last she named. When the church bell rang, she heard it, and she said, "I should have liked to see Stephen Castle once more." You know she felt free to call you so, and you will excuse me that I repeat her words. We asked her if you should be sent for to the funeral, and she shook her head and said, "Too far, don't trouble him;" but she wanted her love given, and she always grieved a good deal that your poor mother died and left you. That was more than a year ago, and Aunt Eliza has failed faster ever since. Aunt Eliza was buried yesterday, and it would have done us good to have heard you speak a few words, but we must not repine.

We shall be glad if you can come and make us a visit some time.

Please excuse these lines, etc., etc.

The lights, the music, the flowers, the beautiful women all seemed to whirl away from Stephen Castle as he read this letter, and he was in a low-roofed farmhouse in Thornton, bending over his old friend, meeting the love-light in her eye before it was quenched forever, catching one last glimpse of her spirit before it fled. It seemed to him that he would have given all that made his life just then to have looked once more into the sweet old face. He had never known, except from his mother, a love so tender, so exalted as Aunt Eliza's, nor one which so uplifted his own nature. She was one of those rare persons who mysteriously touch every soul they meet to its utmost of purity and aspiration. No woman whom he had seen in all this glittering world in which he moved now, was in this way to be compared with her.

"I loved her,— she needed me," the young man cried in his heart, holding the letter crushed in his hand; and a moment after he rose, and, making his way to Mrs. Petersham, excused himself and left the place.

Mr. Loring was in the parquet with a friend, and he watched Stephen as he appeared for a moment in the most conspicuous part of the box, bending with courtly deference to speak to his hostess.

"I tell you," Mr. Loring remarked to his friend, "I never saw anything equal the transformation in that fellow, — Castle, I mean. When he came here he was good-looking enough — he couldn't help being striking, put him anywhere — and talented, you know, a scholar — but that was all. He had been in the country all his life, knew nothing of society, art, music, the ways of the world on any side. He was full of a lot of Puritanic notions, and I thought for a while he would kick out of the traces the best we could do. But bless your heart! inside of a year he settled down to business in great shape, and I certainly never saw a man improve so rapidly in my life. He has travelled, you know; is up on art; hears good music, an opera now and then, — nothing beyond clerical propriety, of course, — preaches elegant sermons, and he can hold his own socially with any clergyman in New York."

"Yes, I hear the ladies are all breaking their hearts over him. He is getting to be the fashion, you might say. Don't they spoil him with all the flattery? He is a young fellow still."

"No, they can't spoil him, and they can't catch him either; that's what amuses me!" said Mr. Loring, laughing; and then the curtain rose, and the conversation ended.

The following morning Stephen Castle was sitting at his study-desk, pen in hand, essaying to write a letter of sympathy to Electa Wescott in Thornton. Her letter lay on the table beside him, and with it a faded, old-fashioned card photograph of Aunt Eliza, which would have signified nothing to a stranger, but in seeing which, Stephen could call up vividly the arch smile, the unconscious grace, the pure sweet-heartedness which had made the little old lady so dear to him. He looked careworn and sad this morning, and the letter was a hard one to write. Presently, as his pen groped its slow way on, he was interrupted by a servant who brought him the letters just delivered by the postman.

Stephen pushed his writing-materials aside, as glad of an occasion for postponing a difficult task, and proceeded to cut open the several envelopes with a silver paper-knife of rare and curious device. His study was large and luxuriously appointed. Costly pictures were upon the walls, many of them gifts from his wealthy parishioners; but in one remote corner hung a photograph of Hunt's "Light of the World," the one link between this study and the one in the little parsonage at Thornton.

One letter which Stephen opened aroused an expression of keener interest than the rest. It was dated at Winchester, the seat of the Divinity School where he had himself graduated, and it was written by a student there who was to be ordained pastor of the church in Thornton in the following June. He wrote in the respectful tone of one addressing a man far above him, — and yet with a manly confidence which pleased Stephen Castle, — to ask if the latter would be present in Thornton at the time of his ordination, and preach the sermon, which was always looked forward to as the event of these occasions.

Stephen turned at once to his desk and wrote a few words of cordial acceptance. Then, taking up a calendar, he wrote on it for the fifth, sixth, and seventh of June the word "Thornton." This done, he sat a long time with his head dropped upon his hand, thinking. The last time he had visited Thornton was on his way home from the burial of his mother, and this circumstance and the death of Aunt Eliza brought his mother very tenderly to his mind. Her life in New York had been a poor, homely little tragedy, not devoid, after all, of some great elements. Where Stephen had gradually yielded to the influence of his environment, she had held herself rigidly apart, and maintained her position of Puritanic soberness. The Church of All Good Spirits had no use for her, this being so, and she distinctly understood this. At Thornton she had had her household cares like other housewives, but she had been considered always as on a plane above all the rest, and was accustomed to being deferred to as a kind of spiritual leader.

Now all was different. In her inmost heart she was convinced that her son was being led away from her, and from "pure religion and undefiled;" and this conviction ate into the very sources of her vital energy. Homesick beyond expression, homeless rather, she felt herself a useless appendage to Stephen's life, instead of being its chief support; and with no word of upbraiding or complaint she pined and failed day after day, so gradually that Stephen did not dream of her growing weakness until the last. Then, with full consciousness, she lay down to die, calm and collected, without triumphs or ecstasies, but with unshaken faith, asking only at Stephen's hands that she be taken back to the little New England village where she was born, and laid to rest beside his father.

Stephen had sent for Emily Merle, who had always been like his mother's right hand in her work in Thornton; and the girl had come and taken her place with the nurse by the bedside, and had remained there until all was over. It was a rest, even now, to recall her sweet, womanly ways, and the quiet sympathy which could make itself felt without words. Rousing suddenly from his attitude of dejection, he pulled his letter to Electa Wescott back to its place before him, and finished it with no further hesitation. At the close he wrote: —

"Yes, I shall make you all a visit before many months. I have promised Mr. Waldo to preach his ordination sermon in June, and I cannot say how glad I am that I can look forward to seeing the people I love so well at that time."

He was addressing the letter when his friend, Lloyd Petersham, came in. After a little conversation of no particular interest, Petersham said, with a troubled expression, —

"Have you seen Mr. Loring this morning?"

"No, I have not been out at all yet."

"I thought he might possibly have been in. You have not heard, then, that Miss Loring is quite ill?"

"No," cried Stephen, much startled; "how can it be so? She was at her very best, apparently, last night."

"I know; I never saw her lovelier or more brilliant;" and young Petersham spoke as if it were pleasant to recall the image of Stephanie as they had seen it so few hours before. "She was taken, it seems, with a severe chill not very long after you left, and went home. She has been alarmingly ill through the night."

Stephen rose and paced the room with unconcealed distress upon his face.

"I will go around there before lunch," he said.

"You cannot expect to see her," said Petersham, thoughtfully.

"No, certainly not, but I can at least know more exactly the state of things."

"What a strange fellow you are, Castle!" said the other, after a little silence.

"How so, Lloyd?"

"Why, do you know I believe you might have had the right to be near her at a time like this! What any other man would die to win you hardly seem to seek."

Stephen changed color perceptibly.

"Don't, Petersham!" he exclaimed.

X.

Falls are not always by the grosser sins which the world takes count of but by spiritual sins, subtle and secret, which leave no stain upon the outward life.

CARDINAL MANNING.

God draws a cloud over each gleaming morn.
    Would we ask why?
It is because all noblest things are born
    In agony.

Only upon some cross of pain or woe
    God's sun may lie;
Each soul redeemed from self and sin must know
    Its Calvary.

FRANCES POWER COBEE.

STEPHEN CASTLE was standing in the broad upper hall of the Lorings' house, which was dimly lighted and profoundly still. Below in the library, he had left Mr. Loring and his wife, with whom he had exchanged a few agitated words. He was waiting now, his head drooping forward, a chilly dampness gathering on his forehead, as he watched a door opposite the place where he stood. It opened at length noiselessly, and a man appeared, who joined him and spoke with

Across the room Stephanie Loring was the centre of a group.

the calmness of the experienced physician in a time of crisis.

"Mr. Castle, I believe? Yes, as I supposed. You understand it is Miss Loring's wish to see you. It is to be regretted," with a deprecatory lifting of shoulders and brows, "on account of her extreme exhaustion, but I suppose we can hardly refuse the request."

Stephen's eyes fell at the suggestion of the doctor's last words, and a tremor ran through his frame which he quickly controlled.

"You do not think it will increase the exhaustion seriously?" he asked.

"Not more than the excitement of having her wish opposed. I do not anticipate an immediate change. You will, of course, avoid any subject which might produce agitation. I depend upon your judgment entirely, Mr. Castle, as Miss Loring wishes to see you alone."

He led the way now to the opposite door, which he softly opened, saying, as he did so, "You may remain about half an hour if it seems best;" and then, Stephen having entered, he closed the door behind him.

For a moment, in the strange hush of the room, the young man stood unable to move forward. It was dark, save for a night-lamp burning at some distance from the door. The air had a peculiar odor, aromatic and yet stupefying. At the foot of the bed a woman in white cap and apron was quietly folding a light blanket, which she laid upon the bed, and then disappeared into an adjoining room.

Then at last Stephen advanced to the bedside, took the chair which had been left there for him, and looked again, for the first time in many weeks, upon the face of Stephanie. He had not seen her since the night of Mrs. Petersham's dinner, when she had been in the perfection of her beauty and power, — gay, witty, brilliant, — a woman of the world with the world at her feet. Now he saw lying on the broad pillows a white shrunken face and figure, the small thin hands lying passively over the coverlet, the lips colorless, the eyes deeply sunken, a woman around whom the shadows of the next world seemed to be gathering thickly. At first Stephen thought he could discover no familiar line or look in the face before him; but when he took the weak hand in his and for an instant pressed it to his lips, there looked out from the eyes something of the old radiance of Stephanie's smile. She seemed to try to speak, but in vain, for no sound came from her lips. In sore anguish Stephen sought the only refuge which seemed left to him, and said in a voice which all the power of his will could not steady, —

"Shall I pray, dear?"

Her eyes did not give the assent for which he looked; but she spoke now, and to his surprise quite clearly, the old familiar inflections of her voice unchanged, in spite of its weakness.

"I do not care," she said; "we have only a little time. I do not feel that it would make any difference, do you?" and the hollow eyes looked searchingly into his.

Stephen's surprise was so great that he did not reply, and she said, —

"Of course it is the proper thing for you to do, but it would not mean much for either of us."

Still Stephen was speechless, with a horror as of something beyond death coming upon him.

"Now, lying here," Stephanie went on feebly, "nothing holds, you see, but the real things. I think you believed in prayer when I knew you first, and I know you think you do now, but the life is gone."

"Stephanie," Stephen spoke at last with exceeding gentleness, "God is for us when we need Him, even though I am cold and weak where I should be strong. No matter how I have failed, God does not fail."

"Yes, yes," she murmured half impatiently, "I cannot stop to argue. I have only a little time, you see. They do not tell me so, but I know by their faces. I thought once that God was so close and real to you that you would bring Him to me, — you understand? I had never found Him and doubted everything — then I saw you, up there in Thornton."

She paused a little; and Stephen, softly smoothing her hand, said, —

"Yes, I remember. You came to church, and afterward I saw you at the wedding."

"Then I was determined to have you come here. I knew I could do it. You do not know why. It was because I thought your religion could stand even here. I needed it. I thought you could give it to me."

"And I have not,' murmured Stephen, wondering, in a consciousness which seemed to overlie the unimaginable abyss of his pain, whether ever priest had heard such a deathbed confession as this.

"No," she said calmly, using in her stress only the necessities of bare truth, — "no, you are like the rest. There is no help, no God, in what you preach. It could not stand, — the life I thought you had; so there is nothing left for me."

"Oh, Stephanie;" and Stephen Castle groaned aloud, disregarding for an instant the danger of exciting her, in the poignancy of his suffering.

"Do not mind," she said tenderly; "life is too much for any of us, I think. I was wrong to expect you to be stronger than men are. Pride and intellect and ambition are what really rule all men; only they call them different names."

Stephen hardly heard what she said; his whole soul was concentrated in an inner cry that God would undo the evil he had wrought.

She had turned her head slightly on the pillow; and when he lifted his eyes, he was startled at the expression with which she was watching him.

"We will not speak any more of all that," she said, smiling faintly. "I have more to tell you, — the other reason why I wanted you to come to us. Perhaps you would never have known it if — I were not so ill; but now, you see, I cannot wait. You must know it. I cannot keep it in my heart to the very end, Stephen;" and there was something so piteous in the appeal of her face and voice, so unlike the proud woman she had always been, that painful tears rushed to Stephen's eyes.

"It was only," and she shielded her face from his eyes with one transparent hand, "that from the very first, with all my life and all my heart, I loved you."

There was a throbbing silence for a moment, which it was impossible for either to break; and then Stephanie said, —

"It is strange for me to tell you this. Life could never have done it; but now what does it matter? It is the one true thing left to me, — all the rest of my life seems meaningless."

Kneeling beside the bed, Stephen drew the wasted form for a moment into his strong arms, and kissed her solemnly on brow and lips.

"God bless you and keep you, dear, and hold you close, and give you light and peace. Amen."

His voice was firm, and there was a strange thrill of hope and power in it; and as he rose to his feet, he seemed to shed upon Stephanie a mysterious grace and benediction.

Then the door opened, the physician, watch in hand, came in with a look of warning on his face, and the clergyman withdrew.

White and haggard and half benumbed with pain, Stephen made his way out of the house and on through the darkness of the night to his own silent rooms. Having struck a light, he glanced mechanically at his own reflection in the glass over his dressing-table, and turned away amazed at the change which the last hour had wrought in his face. There were lines and furrows in it such as only remorse and sorrow cut, but what struck most sharply upon his consciousness was the perception that his face was no longer that of a free man. The look of self-poise, of freedom, of firm will, was gone. It had become an irresolute, tortured face. Strangely enough, with the recognition of this change came the thought that he was glad that Emily Merle could not see him now.

Entering his study, Stephen sat down beside the desk, and with his head bowed between his hands he remained there hour after hour, struggling for a clear comprehension of the point reached in his own experience which had made this interview with Stephanie possible, and of the way along which he had come to it.

A Minister of the World

He did not dwell long upon the later part of their conversation. That she had loved him with the whole power of her nature, and that she had thus confessed her love in the hour of her extremity, gave him just now little personal feeling. Something of consecration and of emotion seemed to rest upon him, even in his pain, from this revelation, but it had no power to hold his thoughts. He had been under the spell of her beauty and charm all the years that he had known her, although some element of his nature had always risen in protest when he would have declared himself her lover. The very delicacy of his feeling now forbade his placing strong emphasis on the fact that it was she who had given voice to the powerful attraction existing between them, rather than himself.

The awful rock upon which his soul seemed crashing in perpetual wreck, repeated through hour after hour of the night, was the fact that he had been pronounced by a soul in the face of death, and to that soul's undoing, faithless to his trust. This, in brief, was to him the import of Stephanie's words, spoken with the awful sincerity of death. She had sought power and faith and guidance in him as in one standing in vital relation to God, and she had found weakness and self-seeking and spiritual confusion. She had seen the desire for power and pre-eminence and intellectual distinction crowding out the devotion to poor and humble souls as those for whom Christ died, which had been the passion of his early ministry. She had seen the crumbling of faith, the weakening of conviction, the subtle admixture of motive. He saw it now with startling clearness, but so gradually had the change come about that not until this hour had he known what manner of man he had come to be. Now, at last, he saw it, and, in bitterness of spirit, he called himself false to God and men, — false to the faith of his fathers, false to the ideals of his youth.

Stephen Castle was no coward. That Stephanie might have known all the way along that it had been her own voice which won him away from the strength and simplicity of his earlier manhood, did not for a moment lessen his sense of responsibility for his own failure, or the gentleness of his feeling for her. What if the loss of faith and power which she met in him were her own work, and work not all blindly wrought, it would still have been impossible for

Stephen to offer this in his own excuse. To captivate, to dazzle, to lead whither she would, was a part of the personality of this woman whose life had touched his in its most impressible years. It had still remained possible for his own nature to reject an influence overstrong, to retain its poise, its freedom. If it had not done this, the fault was in the weakness of the man, not in the power of the woman. This he felt keenly. And it had been once in his hands to lead Stephanie to the life " which is the light of men;" and he, in what seemed to him now unfathomable folly, had, instead, allowed her to lead him into darkness! Nothing was left them now but darkness, — now, when her soul was hovering in the borderland, where death's shadow falls, and his own soul was falling, broken and despairing, upon the thorns of life!

Worn out at last, Stephen fell asleep at his desk, an image from the Inferno vaguely haunting his uneasy sleep, of two troubled spirits flitting, wailing and homeless, through an endless darkness.

On the following Sunday in the Church of All Good Spirits many persons in the congregation observed the extreme pallor of the young pastor as he stood before them in the pulpit, and the very unusual languor of his manner. There were some who attributed these manifestations of suffering to the critical condition of Stephanie Loring, who was still lying, apparently, at the gates of death. There were none who divined the darkness, deeper than any which the shadow of death could bring, in which his soul was wrapped that day. The subdued splendor of the stately building, its impressive architecture, the richness of its wood-carving and stained glass, the noiseless footsteps of the worshippers as they trod the thick carpets of the aisles, their graceful and well-bred devotions, the very flattery in their faces as they looked at himself, — all these things in which before he had found high satisfaction oppressed him unspeakably to-day.

Even the deep tones of the organ jarred upon him; and when the quartette, which was the pride of All Good Spirits and the envy of all other churches of its order, produced a classic selection with marvellously artistic perfection, he longed to break the spellbound attention of the people with the rude discords of which his own soul was full.

Stephen had taken, almost at random, an old

sermon that morning. He had hardly read it through. Not until he announced it did he recognize the bitter irony of the text: " Ye are the salt of the earth ; but if the salt have lost its savor, wherewith shall it be salted ? "

XI.

Out of the place of death,
   Out of the cypress shadow,
Out of sepulchral earth,
   Dust that Calvary gave,
Sprang as fragrant of breath
   As any flower of the meadow,
This, with death in its birth,
   Sent like speech from the grave.

So, in a world of doubt,
   Love — like a flower —
Blossoms suddenly white,
   Suddenly sweet and pure,
Shedding a breath about
   Of new, mysterious power,
Lifting a hope in the night,
   Not to be told, but sure.

                  Madame Darmesteter.

"STEPHANIE will recover!" This sentence was ringing through Stephen Castle's brain like bells of joy, as he walked up and down his study, his haggard face illuminated again with something of the hope and courage which had been absent from it for so many days. Mr. Loring had just left him, having rushed in, almost wild with excitement and the reaction after long suspense, to tell him that the doctors pronounced that the force of Stephanie's disease had spent itself, and that, contrary to all their expectation, her strength had endured the terrible strain, and there was reason to hope that she would recover.

"They say they never saw such elasticity, such rebound, such a superb organization." This Mr. Loring had said to Stephen, unaware himself that tears were running down his cheeks; and he hurried away to give an hour or two to the business interests which for the last few weeks he had utterly ignored.

"Stephanie will recover!" All that this meant to Stephen himself he did not — he could not — consider. His beautiful, peerless friend was given back to life, to the air, to the sun, to freedom, and to joy! The wonderful radiance of her smile was not to be quenched; her beauty and grace and charm were not to be given to the embrace of death. Life, which had seemed of late so bare and joyless, now looked bright again, and Stephen felt all his pulses run full and fast. And yet there was a swift perception which clouded his brow and steadied him in the joyful tumult of the moment. Now, with life and strength coming back, and the ordinary considerations of convention asserting themselves, how would a proud woman like Stephanie feel, in remembering the revelation of her love which she had made to him, Stephen Castle, when she supposed herself to be near the end of life? He felt himself grow hot and cold for her, knowing by intuitive sympathy what she would suffer, and how she would shrink from the recollection which he felt sure would haunt her day and night, even in this time of restoration.

Hardly had this perception made itself clear to his consciousness when Stephen's mind leaped to a solution of the difficulty, — the only natural and adequate solution, he instantly felt. One thing only could reconcile Stephanie to the thought of her confession to him, but that one thing was sufficient. It was that he should ask her to be his wife. A man of a different mental and moral organization would have taken a day to reflect and to decide upon a step like this. A cautious man would have seen serious considerations against it, which must be carefully weighed. For in the past week Stephen had gradually reached the point of believing that the only way back to his integrity as a minister of Christ lay in a complete break from his present surroundings. But all this was impossible to Stephen. No consideration of self, however just at other times, could hold against the instinct of a chivalrous nature in a crisis like this. Stephanie's happiness was clouded, her recovery perhaps retarded, by a humiliation from which it was in his power to save her. He hesitated no more to throw himself into the breach than a knight of King Arthur's time would have stopped to consider his own safety when called upon to do battle for a fair lady.

Within an hour of Mr. Loring's call, a note was on its way to Stephanie in which Stephen Castle said, —

"Will you forgive me that I do not wait, as I ought, until you are stronger, but that now, in my great joy that God is giving you back to us, I dare to ask that to me, more than to all others, you may be given?

"I know, in some faint degree, I think, how surpassingly great is the favor I ask. I know, too, how unworthy I am to ask it; but all that I am or can be is yours if you will take it. Do not try to write or to see me until you are quite strong. I can be patient now."

A day or two passed. There was a great storm at sea, with awful shipwreck and disaster.

As the light of the lamp struck upward on her face, he recognized Emily Merle.

A Minister of the World

Stephen, restless and unable to force himself into any of his wonted occupations, left the city and went out to a little settlement on an exposed point of the Long Island coast, to watch the effects of the storm, and to fight, with the men of the life-saving station, for the lives of shipwrecked sailors who might be washed ashore at that point.

He found something of relief in the struggle of the elements: his own personal conflicts were lost for the time, and he seemed to come into touch with the majestic powers of nature, which even in their fiercest manifestations can quiet the fever and passion of the human heart.

Returning late at night to his apartment, he found, in a pile of letters waiting for him, not the one he half expected from Stephanie, but one from Emily Merle, asking him when he came to Thornton to bring her a certain book which she had sent for in vain to different booksellers.

Stephen started to his feet in consternation. Thornton! To be sure, he was under engagement to go to Thornton the fifth of June to attend Waldo's ordination. The experiences and excitements of the last six weeks had entirely driven the matter from his mind, and now it was the fourth of June. His ordination sermon had not even been thought of, the arrangements for his absence were not made, and yet he must start at seven o'clock the next morning; even then it was doubtful whether he could reach Thornton, which was not on the main line of railroad, the same night.

Stephen turned the leaves of his calendar. Yes, there was no room for doubt in the matter; he had written "Thornton" across the spaces occupied by the next three days. When he had written it, the time had seemed far away. How distinctly it all came back to him now: it was the night at Mrs. Petersham's, the night he had last seen Stephanie Loring in health, the evening he had heard of Aunt Eliza's death. There was no time now to be spent in meditation. He must make ready for his journey. Fortunately the book which Emily wanted was in his own library. It went first into his gripsack, which he at once proceeded to pack, throwing in another book or two to help him in working up his sermon, which he must prepare on the cars. Then he wrote half a dozen hasty notes, arranging for different appointments to be met during his absence; among them was one to Lloyd Petersham, asking him to explain his sudden departure fully to the Lorings, and to attend to the immediate forwarding of any letters which might come to him the next day. Having done all these things, Stephen ordered his breakfast for six o'clock, and lay down for a few hours of sleep.

At eight o'clock the next evening a train, evidently impatient at the necessity, slowed up for half a minute at a little station in a cut between two grassy hills, and having deposited a solitary passenger steamed on again, as if eager to reach a point of greater consequence. The man who alighted, at the station under the hill, was Stephen Castle; and, half a mile to the west, the spire which rose against the pale yellow sky where the sunset fires were burning out, was the spire of the Thornton church.

There was no one there to meet him, no one at the station but the man who had it in charge; and this was what he hoped for and what he expected. Before he left New York in the morning he had telegraphed to Thornton that, the connections being uncertain, he would spend the night at Winchester. He did this knowing that he could join the little party of professors from the Divinity School there who would doubtless attend Waldo's ordination, and with them reach Thornton in time for the morning session of the Council. However, in the course of the day he had found that he could, after all, by availing himself of another road, reach Thornton in the evening. The longing to see the place was growing strong within him, and to see it in its normal quiet, before the influx of visitors to the ordination had transformed it. He knew that some one would give him a bed; and so he came on, without stopping at Winchester.

Leaving his gripsack with the station-master, who recognized him and received him with manifest but silent enthusiasm, Stephen ran up the long flight of steps to the crest of the hill, and struck out on the road which ran between clover-fields up to the village. It was twilight, and the grassy path by the roadside along which he walked was wet with dew. The white farmhouses, each with its company of barns, red or ochre or unpainted gray, lay in unbroken silence, with broad meadows and orchards between. The air was pure as crystal, and sweet with the breath of many blossoms. How still it was! His own footsteps were the only sound except the ripple of the brook as it ran beside the road and under the old bridge. The clear water broke in shallow cascades over the red-brown stones, just as it used in the sweet old time when he was wont to come there Saturday afternoons for the rest and cooling of its music. And the man, the boy rather, eager and free-hearted, who used to linger there was himself, Stephen Castle, who now stood on the little bridge, with care and pain and a bitter sense of failure ever with him. Of course there came the longing to break away from his present conditions and take refuge in a haven of peace like this, but as inevitable was the recognition that this was impossible as well as useless. The time for peace and repose in his life was over, until old age should bring it back perchance; he was in the years of conflict now, and must endure hardness as a soldier.

Stephen left the bridge and passed on by the familiar path. He had reached a farmhouse now where he had always been a welcome guest. He noticed with a smile of pleasure, as he passed the hayfields, that the crop was large and fine. The old satisfaction which he used to share with the Thornton people in "a good year" came back to him. No one was in sight about the house. He was glad and

A Minister of the World

sorry too. He was not quite ready yet to meet his Thornton friends, and yet he longed for such an old-fashioned grasp of the hand as he knew was ready for him. Up the hill now and past the parsonage; but the dusk was deepening, and the house could hardly be seen among its vines and bushes of lilac and syringa. There was a light in the middle room. Stephen supposed Waldo was there. He wondered if he were to be married, or whether he would live with a sister or with his mother, as he had done. The fragrance of the locust blossoms, high in the dark above his head, came to him with the mysterious power over memory which odors possess. All his life in the little parsonage, his mother and her love and devotion, came before him with overmastering power, and his tears flowed unchecked. He leaned for a moment on the parsonage gate. He had thus far met not a single person; but a boy was coming down the gravel walk from the direction of the post-office now, and Stephen stood aside to let him pass.

He was not ready yet to go into the parsonage, and find Waldo, and explain his presence in Thornton to-night. He would rather walk on. A few steps more and he saw a faint light shining through the windows at the farther end of the church. Perhaps he could slip in unobserved and have a few moments alone in the stillness there to calm and collect himself. The door was closed, but opened readily when he tried it; and he found no one in the narrow vestibule, which was unlighted. He knew his way well, and in a moment had climbed the steep stairs to the choir gallery, the door of which he cautiously opened. The church was dark except for one lamp on the communion table at the opposite end. Unseen, he entered the gallery and sat down in the shadow of the organ.

At first he thought there might be no one in the building but himself; but an instant later he perceived that a woman's form was bending over some jars of flowers near the pulpit, and suddenly, as she lifted her head and the light of the lamp struck upward on her face, he recognized Emily Merle. His heart gave a great leap of joy, and a strange warmth and comfort and release from pain seemed to flow through his consciousness. What power of healing and uplift lay in a womanhood so strong and steadfast, — in a nature which had never spent itself on the semblances of life, but had

had to do with its truths! Like a cooling draught in his fever and pain, Stephen felt the girl's presence. What would have befallen her in "the great world," as they called it, — the world in which he had lost his path and his purpose full soon? Was it only the accident of environment which had made Emily Merle what she was? No, Stephen made answer to himself: the high integrity of her spiritual life would have stood the proof, as his, too, might have done, for the stern word of the great moralist came back to him in the silence: "It always remains true that if we had been greater, circumstances would have been less strong against us."

She was busy with flowers and ferns, and moved about quietly, but with evident absorption in her work, sometimes stepping back a few paces to note the effect, then returning to lift a vine or turn a flower with dainty touch. All her attitudes were unconsciously graceful, and there was a sweet seriousness in her face, and a womanly dignity in her bearing which Stephen had never recognized as he did now.

He heard a door below him swing after a moment, and Emily's voice called, —

"Did you find them?"

A Minister of the World

"Yes, there were plenty, and very good ones." The two voices reverberated strangely through the empty church.

A young girl now came into the circle of light around the pulpit, and Stephen saw that her hands were full of tall ferns, which she gave to Emily.

Five, ten minutes passed as if in a dream to Stephen alone in his shadowed place, and memories of his youthful ministry clustered close about him. The dark church with its one little circle of light, which seemed strangely far away, the grotesque shadows cast by the single lamp, the quiet voices and movements of the two girls as they handled the ferns whose shadows were like trees as they flitted across the walls, all made up an impression of unreality, and he ceased to know or care where he was or why he was there. Presently he heard a voice say, —

"I wonder if he will be the same."

It was Emily Merle's voice which answered,

"No, he is not the same."

"Do you mean that he has grown proud and will look down upon people like us?" the voice asked again.

"No, not that; he could never be like that.

His heart is as true as steel. You will find him kinder than ever, and interested in us as he used to be. But, after all, it is different." There was a little silence, and then Emily Merle added, —

"He does not belong to us any more, you see, and he never can again."

Stephen was awake now, and alive to the fact that it was he of whom they were speaking. Was it the distance, or was he right in thinking that there was a pathetic note in Emily's voice, an undertone of sadness? An impulse he could hardly control swept over him to go to her that moment, and look into her face, and tell her that he did belong to her, and to her only. He knew it now, and understood what had kept him all these years from other love. Then, even as he had risen impulsively and stood in the dark shadows of the gallery as if doubting what to do, a sudden recollection came to him, and noiselessly as he had entered it, he left the church and came out alone into the summer night.

He had, until that moment, forgotten Stephanie.

XII.

The world's infections; few bring back at eve,
Immaculate, the manners of the morn.
Something we thought, is blotted; we resolved,
Is shaken; we renounced, returns again.
YOUNG.

"YES, Waldo, you will find them a loyal, united people, unless they have greatly changed in the years since I left here, — a good people to work with, and Thornton is a good place if you want to study."

It was Stephen Castle speaking. He and Waldo were sitting at a bare, round table on which stood a small lamp in the midst of a variety of miscellaneous articles. They were in the sitting-room of the Thornton parsonage, which was a scene of the complete confusion incident to the early stage of settling a new home. In the little room which had formerly been Stephen's study, there stood an old-fashioned sofa of liberal size, on which he was to sleep, while Waldo would make a bed for himself on the parlor floor. Stephen had been in the house for half an hour, and it had taken nearly all that time to reconcile with Waldo's overflowing hospitality his objections to letting so distinguished a guest share such poor accommodations as were just now at his disposal. He had proposed to take Stephen to the farmhouse where he was expected to stay the following night; but Stephen begged so earnestly for the favor of sleeping one night under the parsonage roof that Waldo yielded, although with many misgivings. They were now spending an hour in discussing Thornton and Waldo's prospects in his first field of labor, the younger man listening to Stephen's words as if each one were of profoundest weight. He was a short, slender fellow, Waldo, with straight black hair and dark eyes, a thoughtful face, and a way of speaking which gave an impression of almost intense sincerity.

"Yes, I know I shall be happy here," he remarked now, in response to Stephen's words. "Nelson, you know, who followed you, had a very good pastorate here. He is abroad now, studying."

"Yes, I have kept track of his movements. He is a good fellow. He had a family, I believe, had he not?"

"Yes, a wife and one child. The parsonage has not been used since they left."

"How is it with you, Waldo? Are you going to housekeeping? These preparations look like it," Stephen remarked pleasantly.

"Oh, yes," replied the other, smiling brightly, "my sister is coming next week to take care of me. I have no prospect of anything further than that, Mr. Castle, at present."

For a moment Stephen thought of Emily Merle over there in the church at work among the flowers, and a vision of what might be filled him with an almost fierce desire to thwart such a possibility; but he only said half carelessly:

"There is plenty of time for all that sort of thing. One thing at a time. A man's ordination is enough of an event for one year."

"Is it not, indeed?" cried Waldo, an expression of something like awe coming into his face. "This is my last night before it, you know, and I am sure you understand what my feeling must be. It seems so glorious a privilege, in one way, to be dedicated to the one single life work, to belong solely to Christ and to carrying His message; but then, on the other hand, it is almost appalling to me. The responsibility seems so enormous, the fear that the consecration may not be complete comes continually. Were you ever troubled in such a way, Mr. Castle?" and the young man looked appealingly into Stephen's eyes.

The latter could only bow his head.

"I am afraid it is presuming of me to ask such questions of a man like you, who are so far beyond me in every way," Waldo continued diffidently; "I know it must seem weak and cowardly to you. It is not that I fear that too much is exacted of outward sacrifice and all that. I think I need not say that I have counted the cost, and have left all. I do not even feel this part to be a sacrifice. It does not seem as if death itself for Him would be hard," and as he spoke the earnestness of the young face witnessed to his sincerity, and Stephen found it hard to meet his look; "but what I feel is my own unworthiness to enter so high a calling: the danger that I may bring reproach upon His name, even," and his voice fell and his face clouded, "that I might at heart seek myself in my work, instead of His will and the uplifting of men."

Stephen murmured a half-articulate response, for Waldo's words were like a sword piercing his soul.

"Mr. Castle," the young man asked humbly, "you have gone far beyond me in knowledge and experience. I know through the people here how exalted your spiritual life has always been. May I ask you, because you are past dangers and temptations like these, to pray for me, that I may be saved from them, weak as I know myself to be?"

Stephen could not meet a request like this with mere assent. He was honest. Rising from the table, he held out his hand and took that of Waldo, who saw with surprise the expression of his face.

"I will pray for you, my dear fellow, you may be sure. The dangers you speak of are real dangers. I have met them, and the victory has not always been mine, as you suppose. Good-night! I believe I am tired;" and he took the candle which was ready for him, and abruptly went to his room.

Waldo, left to himself, reflected that this abruptness was, perhaps, a touch of the *grand seigneur* manner which one must expect in successful men, but of which he had until now seen nothing in Mr. Castle, and himself made ready for the night.

It was the following evening, and the Thornton church was crowded to the doors. From all the country side the farmers' families had driven over to the ordination ceremonies, and even more especially to hear Stephen Castle preach. He had been a favorite among church-going people far and wide, when he was the young pastor in Thornton; now he had become a noted city preacher, and great was the curiosity to see and hear him. From Pembroke and all the neighboring villages, large numbers of the clergy and more prominent laity had come; and Winchester had contributed its delegation of theologians, who with their grave and dignified presence had lent impressiveness to the exercises of the day.

The order of the evening was the formal consecration of the candidate, young Waldo, to the ministry of Christ, by the laying on of hands. After this ceremony, noble and affecting in its simplicity, Stephen Castle was to preach.

His whole environment was surcharged with suggestions of his past. Around him sat the venerable professors from Winchester, under whose training his own preparation for the ministry had been made, and a number of clergymen who had been his friends in the days of his Thornton pastorate, stalwart men with manly faces. At his right, and so near that his hand could have touched him, was Waldo, with the high consecration of the hour visible in his face, a face made strangely beautiful by the man's spirit. In him Stephen seemed to see his own former self, before he had been forced to "travel daily farther from the east," and to see the " vision splendid " of his youth " fade into the light of common day."

Before him, among the solid mass of men and women whose faces were turned expectantly to him, were his old friends, true and tried; plain, simple-hearted folk who had faithfully loved him, and loved and honored him still, far, he felt, beyond his due. Almost hidden by the bowers of greenery which her hands had fashioned in the spaces at the side of the pulpit, to conceal the bareness of the walls, sat Emily Merle.

XIII.

> Though thou loved her as thyself,
> As a self of purer clay,
> Though her parting dims the day,
> Stealing grace from all alive;
> Heartily know,
> When half-gods go,
> The gods arrive.   EMERSON.

AS he stood, during the singing of "Coronation" which preceded the sermon, Stephen had looked at Emily, whom he had hardly been able to speak with all through the day, and in a strange flash of imagination or perception, he hardly knew which it might be, the personality of Stephanie Loring came before him, as if the two women stood together in his sight, and in themselves showed forth the two influences which had ruled his life. Both were beautiful, both corresponded to powerful instincts of his nature, but how widely they differed! In Stephanie, Stephen saw a full and perfect manifestation — in its relation to personality — of art; while in Emily was as clear an embodiment of truth.

With Stephanie, all the natural resources of life were means adapted to an end, and that end, beauty, harmony, delight, — a fair end and well attained, — the proper aim of art. Art was in her face, in her voice, in her conversation, her motions, her dress, her intellectual activities; in fine, in all that belonged to her and that surrounded her. And in that expression of harmony and beauty he had found pleasure of a high quality; but the one thing which he had failed to find was satisfaction.

In Emily Merle, Stephen recognized the very opposite type of womanhood. Truth was the vital principle, the ruling force in her nature and in her life. Not truth in cold, bare outlines, but made warm and radiant by a loving, womanly nature, endued with an endless capacity for giving itself for others. As certain elements in his own nature had leaped to meet the wonderful charm of Stephanie, when he saw her first in his boyish inexperience, so now, but with far greater power, did other and deeper elements rise to the sense of beauty in the character of Emily Merle. But Stephen held himself in hand. The thought of Stephanie was always with him now, and he knew himself to be pledged to her, and no longer free to

A Minister of the World

yield to the influence of another woman. He could not regret the step which he had taken, it had belonged to the very nature of things, but he saw in the life before him hopeless confusion.

Aroused from the condition of intense introspection into which he had fallen, by the cessation of the music and the rustle of garments as the congregation resumed their seats, Stephen came forward, a hush of eager expectancy pervading the house.

The text which he announced consisted of but three words: "Who emptied Himself." It was not the text which he had selected the day before on his journey to Thornton, nor the sermon which he had then elaborated out of philosophical and poetical elements, after his present method of sermon making, and with perhaps more thought for the Doctors of Divinity who would hear him than for the rustic folk of his old church. In the preceding night, after his interview with Waldo, Stephen had found that to preach that sermon had become an impossibility. A profound desire had taken possession of him to fling aside forever the artificial methods, in which the æsthetic and the literary predominated, and to return to the simple preaching

A Minister of the World

of a simple gospel. And to-night he did it. More than to others he was preaching to himself, with searching and deliberate directness.

The country people, who were awaiting a brilliant display of rhetoric, and dramatic oratory, listened at first with a distinct sense of disappointment. The learned men around him praised him in their hearts for the restraint and simplicity of his speech, realizing the temptation to sacrifice these to the desire to produce a strong personal impression. But as Stephen approached the close of his sermon, the disappointment of the one class and the approval of the other were alike forgotten in the overmastering power of his utterance. Never before had he spoken as he spoke to-night; perhaps never would he again, for this was the supreme hour of crisis in his life, the flood-tide of his experience. All the despair, the remorse, and the humiliation which in the past weeks he had suffered; all the conflict and battle he had waged with the baser elements of his own soul; all the profound sorrow with which he mourned his failure, and his sharp condemnation of the unconscious selfishness of his purposes; all his fresh aspiration for purer service and a single aim, — were fused into the solemn challenge of soul to soul, with which he closed. His form seemed to assume a power beyond itself; his face was touched by a spiritual light which made it "as it had been the face of an angel." It was the hour of the return to truth and unity of purpose of a great soul, greatly confused and gone astray.

Afterward Stephen said that he did not preach that sermon, he experienced it.

Breathless, the congregation sat for a moment, and then together rose and sang, —

> "The Son of God goes forth to war
> A kingly crown to gain."

The service was over, the excitement of receiving hundreds of eager men and women who had pressed to the pulpit stairs to touch his hand had reached its height and subsided, and Stephen stood leaning against a pillar, spent in nerve and brain with the tension of the past hour. A little knot of people still surrounded him, but the church was nearly empty and the hour was late.

Lina Barry, married now, had brought her sleepy, flaxen-haired boy; and her mother and a few others lingered still, among them Mrs. Wescott. As of old, she had more to say than the others.

"I'll tell you jest what it is, now, Elder Castle," she began; "you know I always did have to speak out, and you won't mind me." Here she paused to flash a roguish challenge at Stephen from her black eyes, which were as bright as ever, in spite of the deep lines which the years had cut around them.

"No, I won't mind you," Stephen smiled back languidly.

"Well, when you first begun, and after you'd gone on for quite a piece, thinks I, 'Well, now, I don't know — I guess, after all, Elder Castle don't beat our little minister. He can come up to this.' But by and by you got to goin' along there where you brought in about layin' aside every weight, and all that, and I tell you I had to give in then! I never heard anybody preach in my life like that. You preached me right off the seat!"

At this moment Emily Merle came up to the little group, and "Lec" paused in her voluble speech. Emily had a letter in her hand, which she held out to Stephen.

"Some of the men have been up to the post-office," she said quietly, "and this letter has come for you."

Stephen took the letter in his hand. The

envelope was large and square, and bore a crest upon the seal. The handwriting of the address was altered by physical weakness, but he knew it to be that of Stephanie. Excusing himself to his friends, he left the church as quickly as he could, but not before Emily Merle had seen that he had grown white to the lips.

XIV.

We must learn to look upon life as an apprenticeship to a progressive renunciation, a perpetual diminution in our pretensions, our hopes, our powers, and our liberty. The circle grows narrower and narrower; we began with being eager to learn everything, to see everything, to tame and conquer everything, and in all directions we reach our limit — *non plus ultra*. . . . We have to make ourselves small and humble, to submit to feel ourselves limited, feeble, dependent, ignorant, and poor, and to throw ourselves upon God for all. . . . It is in this nothingness that we recover something of life, — the divine spark is there at the bottom of it. Resignation comes to us, and in believing love we reconquer the true greatness.

AMIEL.

"YOU are noble and knightlike, and I reverence you. My heart thanks you for what you offer, but it is not to be. Your love would be loyal, but it would be cold forever, for it is not possible for a nature like yours to respond fully to mine.

"Let us be satisfied. It is much to have known each other.

"I am stronger, and shall sail soon for a Mediterranean port. I may be away a year. When I return I shall hope to see you again. Till then, good-by.

"STEPHANIE."

A Minister of the World

This was the letter which Stephen Castle opened and read, when, after repeated delays, he at last gained the seclusion of the best bedroom of the farmhouse where he was to spend the night.

His tears fell upon the sheet as he read. She was wise, his beautiful, clear-eyed friend. His heart justified her words, but it ached for the sharp break which they commanded, and for the sense, which can never come to a human heart without pain, that " the old order changeth."

Stephen read the letter over the second time and the third, and reverently kissed the name "Stephanie" at the close; then, no less reverently and tenderly, he held the folded sheet in the flame of his candle, until it turned to a film of ashes and crumbled from his fingers into dust. As he watched the paper shrivel and fall, Stephen felt, rather than promised, that no human being should ever learn from him this phase of the relation between himself and Stephanie. They had been good friends, nothing more.

The next morning he met Emily Merle before the church (he was not inclined to hurry away from Thornton as he would have been before receiving Stephanie's letter), and said, —

"There is a walk that you and I must take together, Emily. Let us go now."

"Where is it? To the Hollow Rocks? That used to be your favorite walk, I remember," Emily responded. She was looking as bright and radiant as the June morning, as she stood under the old maple-trees which guarded the church.

"Yes, you ever-superior young woman. With your usual discernment, you have dived into the recesses of my being and dragged out its profoundest intentions," and they walked on through the village street, talking gayly, Emily giving an unspoken consent to Stephen's wish. Her hands were full of flowers, still fresh, from the decorations of the church, which she told him she must take to two or three house-bound old women who had been unable to share in the great event of yesterday.

"You are still the guardian angel of the parish, I see, Emily," Stephen said, as he took a basket of roses from her hand. "I will go with you and see the poor old bodies. Perhaps they will still remember me."

"Remember you! Why, they talk of you as if you were next of kin to the angels. You cannot understand, Mr. Castle, how our Thornton people adore you. I am sure I don't see why they should," Emily added mischievously.

"You have not forgotten to be disrespectful, I see," laughed Stephen; "and you just now transgressed a plain compact which exists between us when you called me Mr. Castle. Please do not let it occur again, as the professors used to say to us in college after we had committed some undergraduate crime."

"Very well," replied Emily, in her firm, clear-cut fashion of speech, which in its freedom from consciousness Stephen found peculiarly pleasing. "But I started to say that it is so unreasonably hard for these men to follow you here in Thornton. No matter how faithful a man may be, or how well he may preach, the people simply say, 'But he is not Elder Castle!' and the poor man is condemned, — as if he wanted to be Elder Castle, or could be if he would!"

"But Waldo, it is different with him? I am sure the people have taken him into their hearts, as they ought to. He is a thoroughly fine fellow. Don't you think so, Emily?"

"Oh, yes, indeed, but still — he is not Elder Castle!" and with a bright color in her cheeks Emily looked up archly at Stephen, and they laughed together, the spontaneous laughter of two persons who find perfect content in each other's presence.

They had reached the first cottage now where Emily's flowers were to be delivered, and so went in together and sat for a few moments in the dull, low-ceiled room which their presence seemed almost miraculously to brighten to its pain-worn inmate. Other calls followed, and the dew was off the grass, and the sun high, and the shade refreshing, when they reached the cool recesses of the glen known as the "Hollow Rocks," where the Thornton River pauses in its noisy course to fill a silent pool, shut in by pine-trees and great masses of mossy rock.

It had been a favorite place with Stephen when he lived in Thornton, and he threw himself upon the gray old boulder which had been his especial resting-place in those days, with a sigh of satisfaction, while Emily found a niche in the rock just above him, where she made herself comfortable.

"Do you know, my little friend, I begin to believe that there is something in the Antæus myth, as there usually is in the fables of those old Greeks? I am willing to assert that there is positive virtue in this contact with the earth, and, by the same token, with primitive forces in other kinds."

"Primitive folks, for instance!"

"Yes, primitive folks, too, if you please, like Emily Merle." Then, with a sudden gravity which she found by a glance in his face was not assumed, he continued half musingly, —

"Would it surprise you, I wonder, to know how much I have needed a renewal of strength? Perhaps you did not know that I have been a melancholy failure as pastor of All Good Spirits?"

"No! I supposed you had been a brilliant success."

"Ah, Emily, I beg you never to use those words again of me or of any other Christian minister! They are not according to your own thought. You have borrowed them from the phraseology which belongs to a special modern misconception of the ministry. To be brilliant, that is, to make yourself felt to your last reserves, and as much more as you can borrow; to be successful, that is, to have crowds come to hear you and praise you and dine you and wine you and flatter you, — that is the *fin de siècle* ideal of success in the ministry of Christ with a large class of church-going people."

A Minister of the World

"Oh, but no, Stephen! I cannot believe that is true."

"Naturally you cannot, and it is not true of the church at large. Do not misunderstand me. I only tell you what I know to be true in certain circles, and I know of what I speak only too well. The result is, the man becomes at heart an egoist. Either this, or he is truly great, — greater than I can ever be;" and Emily saw with keen sympathy the unfeigned sadness and humility in Stephen's face. She could not reply, and he went on, —

"Such a man as I speak of is simply a man of the world, in a good sense of course. Art, fashion, society, music, the drama, the latest literature of all nations, philosophy, poetry, economics, politics, — all these and all else that goes to make up the life of the world, he must know and use. The old word of Paul, 'I determined not to know anything among you save Jesus Christ and Him crucified,' is translated sometimes in the church of to-day, as the motto for its leader, 'I determined to know everything among you save Jesus Christ and Him crucified.'"

"Did you comprehend this in the beginning of your pastorate of All Good Spirits?"

"In part; and I went in to win. I felt myself strong, and even longed, in a way, to try my strength. My thought was to make the church over, to purify and exalt it."

"But you found it impossible?"

"For a man of my temperament, hopelessly so. It was I who was made over, Emily, until I became altogether such as the rest. Practically our church life is an elevated form of club life, in which the moral and intellectual and æsthetic lines are cultivated, and the members are held together by a kind of social cohesion, awfully unlike the sweet old notion of fellowship in Christ."

"But, Stephen, you must have gained something from this experience. The time cannot have been all lost, nor the effort."

"That is true. In certain ways I have gained much. I have learned, what I should never have learned elsewhere, to have sympathy for the peculiar temptations and characteristics of the fashionable and aristocratic class which belongs to our modern civilization just as it has to every other. Undoubtedly it is in the divine economy that this leisure class should exist, if for nothing else, to furnish employment for the strata below it by the multitude of its artificial needs."

"But there are lovely people among them, — people like Miss Loring, for instance."

"Yes, I have found many unselfish and noble spirits in my church, as far as their personal qualities are concerned, — persons of exquisite fibre. But after all it is hot-house life. They are like exotics. Their development is not along natural lines. Their needs are artificial; their outlook upon life and its demands is utterly unreal. They see it all as through a colored light. Almost unconsciously they come to feel that the world exists for them; not they for the world and its needs, according to the Christian theory."

"And perhaps they are no more to blame than others are for their especial misconceptions."

"That is just. There are many ways in which I have learned of my people what has greatly enriched my life. We must admit, Emily, that what were in some sort the crowning virtues of our fathers are no longer according to the all-powerful Time Spirit, — the rigid austerity, the merciless intensity of conviction, and the intolerance which they produced! I shall never be again the man who used to preach in the church yonder, nor do I wish to be. I am glad for the experiences which have softened my nature and broadened my charity. My poor mother could not go through with the process of transition; it simply was fatal to her. But the change was inevitable. The Puritan mould, intact as it has been kept in our line, is broken in me; nor do I deplore it, except as a matter of sentiment, unless with the narrowness I were to lose the integrity and strength. The men of the last century did their work well. Another type of men is needed now to do the work of the world, of extensive rather than intensive moral quality, with wider sympathies, and with a faith built upon the universal human needs, not upon the conception of an individual or a class."

"I have felt this, even here."

"Of course you have, because you think for yourself, and are ready to see the truth, even if it declares war upon our old traditions. However, we have reached a point now where I can tell you that I am on the point of preparing my resignation as pastor of All Good Spirits."

"It does not greatly surprise me now, although it seems sudden."

"It is less so than it seems. It must have come, but certain things have precipitated it; that young pastor of yours helped, with that

A Minister of the World

pure face of his, and the questions he had to ask me the other night. Of course I could go back and try it over, but I see how it would result. The side of my nature to which the spirit of my present church appeals is too strong to play with. I do not trust myself. There is just one work which I believe I dare to try to do, which I believe God means to give me, if I am not unworthy to continue in His service."

"And tell me what it is, — this work."

"It is in lower New York, Emily; but you do not know what that means. You read of the 'submerged tenth,' and you see a few poor folks here in Thornton with all the sweet air and sunshine in the world to live in, and you try to imagine what the poverty in great cities is, but you cannot. It means much that is very pitiful and desperately brave; but it means too evil which flaunts, not hides itself. But that is the life into which, by the grace of God, I intend to go, and in which I shall remain. I worked the problem out last night. It took all night to do it, because I knew what it meant, you see, and I do not love vice and dirt and the sight of suffering."

"It is not well to sacrifice for the sake of

sacrificing, Stephen." Emily said this with luminous eyes, looking unafraid into his.

"You have put your finger on a point of danger, my dear girl, but I believe I have not made that mistake. No, I am not seeking to atone for the years in which, as Newman says, 'pride ruled my will.' There is nothing of the ascetic in my nature. It is this way: All the years that I have been in All Good Spirits I have wondered what the Lord was going to do about the dark side of the city. I could not help knowing the conditions down there, physical and moral, and at intervals I would be forced to ask myself why it might not be my duty to throw myself into that same work. Plainly the need was crying. However, I always escaped the question in one way or another. Now I have decided that it is the work for me to do."

"But has the work a definite shape? Have you some practical line on which to work?"

"Yes. There is a poor little half-deserted chapel down in Forsyth Street, which I know of, where a spasmodic kind of work has been done. I have some money myself, and I can command more. I know I can get the chapel, and I know I can get decent rooms close by the hardest neighborhood in that region, where I can live. Is that sufficiently definite?" and Stephen, who had risen and was helping Emily down from her seat, looked fondly into her face.

"Yes, I think that will do," she said.

"Does it sound very hard to you?" he asked, as they pushed their way out through interlacing branches to the road.

"Not too hard," was the reply.

He stopped her a moment at the wood's edge, and taking her hands said simply, —

"If God lets me do this work, and some day I come back to ask you, do you think you could do it too?"

"I believe I could," Emily answered with sweet gravity; and they walked back toward the village, not as they had come, but silently.

XV.

And we whose ways were unlike here,
　May then more neighboring courses ply;
May to each other be brought near,
　And greet across infinity.
MATTHEW ARNOLD.

All truly consecrated men learn little by little that what they are consecrated to is not joy or sorrow, but a divine idea and a profound obedience, which can find their full outward expression, not in joy, and not in sorrow, but in the mysterious and inseparable mingling of the two.
PHILLIPS BROOKS.

ON a midwinter Sunday night, a year and a half after that June day in Thornton, Stephen Castle is preaching to a motley crowd in the little down-town chapel of which we heard him speak. The atmosphere of the room is neither pure nor fragrant. The floors are bare, the pews plain benches, and the speaker stands upon a small platform destitute of a pulpit. Many of the faces before him are hard. In the corner by the right of the platform a choir of a dozen girls is gathered around a cabinet organ. These girls have an air of intelligent self-possession which shows that some refining influence has been at work among them, nor is this influence far to seek. Among them, as their leader, with the pure brow and clear eyes we remember, sits the wife of Stephen Castle, Emily, his joy and crown of life, and his spirited co-worker.

While a hymn is being sung before the sermon, the door opens, and a lady, attended by a maid, enters the chapel. Stephen Castle does not see the stranger as she enters, but she is seen and recognized by one person in the room. There is but one woman whom Emily Castle has ever seen whose form and movements have the peculiar grace which marks the new-comer; and although she cannot distinctly see her face beneath its veil, she knows it to be her husband's old friend, Stephanie Loring, now the wife of Lloyd Petersham. She has been married while abroad, and Emily has heard of her recent return to New York, but neither she nor Stephen has met her.

Stepping forward at the close of the hymn to the edge of the platform, Stephen, with a small Testament in his hand, reads a few verses from the Sermon on the Mount. Hardly has he read the verses when his eye, accustomed now to the rough-hewn type of feature of his chapel hearers, notes that other face, and he knows that after many months he is again face to face with Stephanie. A ray of uncontrollable joy in the recognition crosses his face; but as he goes on to interpret the passage chosen, it is plain that he is neither stimulated nor troubled by her presence; in fact, it is for the time forgotten with every other personal consideration. There is no disorder nor inattention in the room. Every eye is riveted upon the face of the preacher; and the love, which in so unusual a degree had been his both among the simple folk in Thornton and the cultured people in the Church of All Good Spirits, is seen in the unwonted gentleness which softens the faces of his hearers.

This experiment has not failed. The highest gifts are not too high for use in uplifting the lowliest, and all the grace and power and energy of Stephen Castle's nature are at work here among the degraded and outcast, and are rewarded.

At the close of the service he and Stephanie meet, with a warm clasp of the hand. Then there are a few cordial inquiries concerning the events and changes which the time of Stepha-

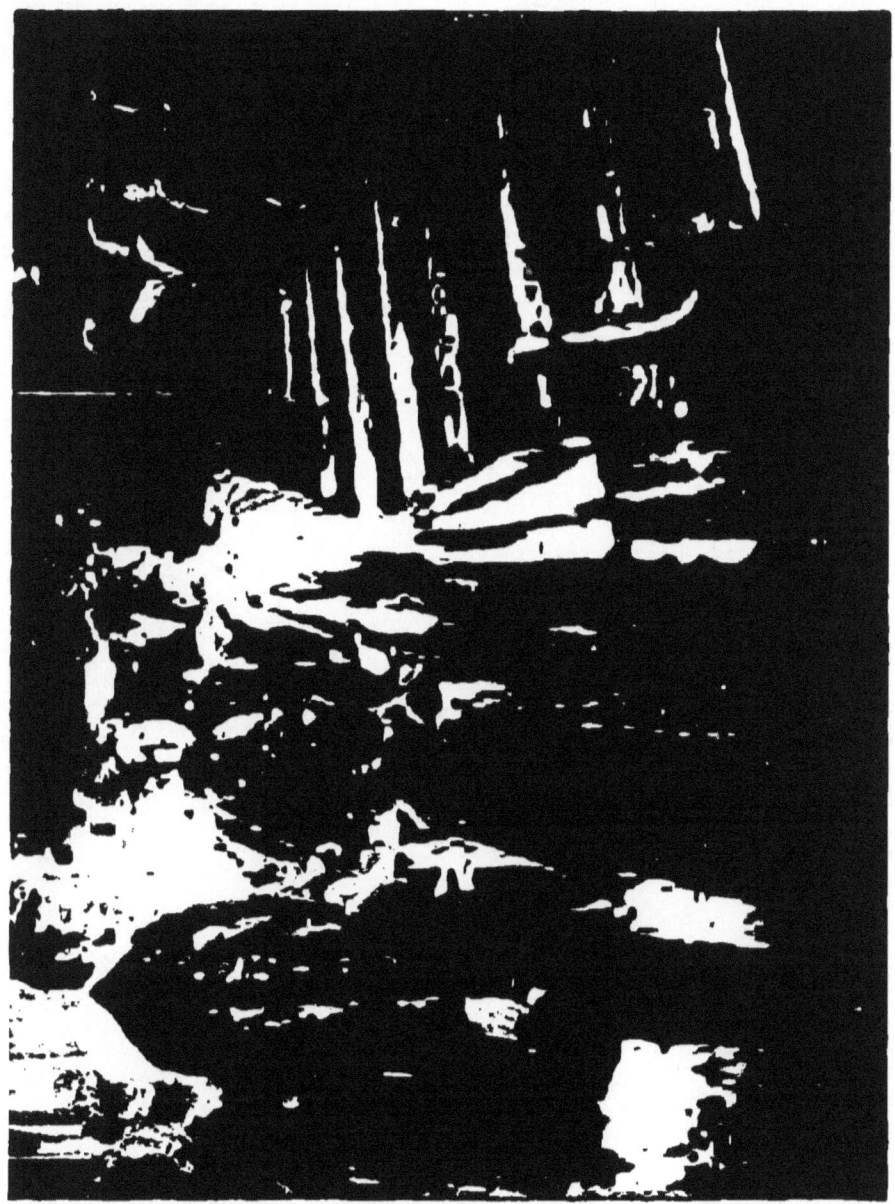

nie's absence has brought, — her recovery, her marriage and his, and many other things. Emily joins them, and the women meet with unaffected kindness. It is not until then that Stephen realizes how greatly Stephanie has changed.

The lights in the chapel are extinguished, and the three come out together into the frosty street, where a carriage is waiting. For a moment Stephanie pauses on the threshold, and Stephen remains beside her.

He has a word for her alone.

"You will let me say, will you not, how glad I was to know of your marriage? Petersham is the noblest fellow!" Stephen speaks low and earnestly.

"Yes, we care for each other very truly. I am satisfied, and I believe he is. Is not that enough? You will come to the house, I hope, and bring your wife. She is a beautiful woman."

"It was kind of you to seek us out away down here. I thank you for coming."

"I wanted to see for myself," she says. "I thought you were mistaken in this hard, hard thing you have done, but I find I was the one mistaken. You have done well."

A Minister of the World

"It is much to me to have you say this." Stephen speaks as one deeply moved.

"Yes, I know. It must be so. Once I hurt you. I was cruel, but you forgave me. All that I said then I can unsay now. When I heard you preach to-night, I believed in you and in the Christ you preached. Good-night."

Having thus spoken, Stephanie enters her carriage; Stephen joins Emily, and under the winter sky they go their different ways.

THE END.

www.ingramcontent.com/pod-product-compliance
Lightning Source LLC
Chambersburg PA
CBHW030254170426
43202CB00009B/739